THE TOWPATH GUI
No.3

CU00811228

A TOWPATH GUIDE TO THE
STOURBRIDGE CANAL

A TOWPATH GUIDE TO THE

Stourbridge Canal

J. IAN LANGFORD

BSc(Eng), PhD, DSc, MIEE
Chartered Engineer
Reader in Powder Diffraction
University of Birmingham

LAPAL PUBLICATIONS

Lapal Publications
53 Senneleys Park Road,
Birmingham B31 1AE,
England

First Published 1992

© J. Ian Langford

ISBN 0 9509238 3 1

Printed in Great Britain by Wolverley Press & Studio Ltd, Cradley Heath.
Tel: (0384) 67541

Contents

Preface   3

1 THE STOURBRIDGE CANAL   5
A brief history

2 THE STOURBRIDGE MAIN LINE   9
Black Delph to Stourton Junction

3 THE STOURBRIDGE BRANCH   23
Stourbridge Wharf to Wordsley Junction

4   THE FENS BRANCH   29
Leys Junction to Brockmoor Basin

5   THE STOURBRIDGE EXTENSION CANAL   33

6   RESTORATION AND CONSERVATION   39

7   ROUTE MAPS   43

APPENDIX   53
The Staffordshire & Worcestershire Canal Society

INDEX   57

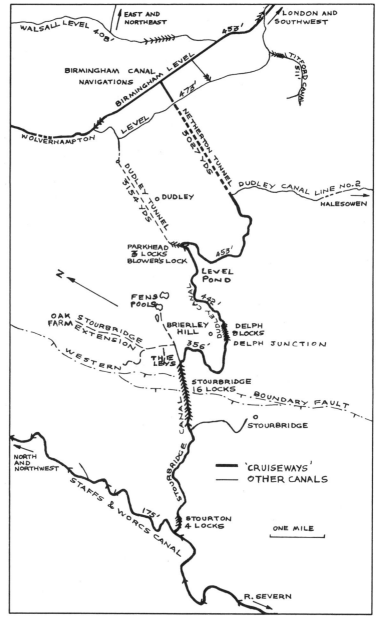

Fig. 1. The Stourbridge Canal and Adjoining waterways

2

Preface

The Towpath Guide to the Stourbridge Canal is a revised and expanded version of a description of the canal in the booklet to commemorate its bicentenary, published in 1979. Other guides in the series are concerned with canals which are mainly rural in character, but the environs of the Stourbridge are largely urban. Also, the mileage covered is considerably less; the entire Stourbridge system is only 7½ miles in length, but it is nevertheless an important link in the Midland waterway network and each mile is full of interest. The Stourbridge Extension Canal is included (Chapter 5), but is not considered in detail, since industrial development has obliterated the greater part of it.

Canals are living history; they are almost unique in providing an unbroken link between the Industrial Revolution of the latter part of the 18th century and the 'Recreational Revolution' of the present. In order to relate what can be seen today, from a boat or the towpath, with the past, a brief history of the Stourbridge is included (chapter 1). A more detailed account is given in Charles Hadfield's *Canals of the West Midlands* (David & Charles, Newton Abbot, 1966).

Throughout its life as a commercial waterway, the Stourbridge was a highly successful enterprise and, aside from a bleak period immediately after nationalisation in 1948, its story as a recreational asset has been equally successful. Indeed, the fact that we now have a national cruising network, preserved in perpetuity, is due in no small measure to events on the Stourbridge. This important phase in the history of the canal is summarised in Chapter 6.

As with earlier Towpath Guides, a system of strip maps (Fig.2, page 43) with varying scale has been adopted to indicate where items of interest may be found, since this allows for changing density of noteworthy features along the canal. These maps are best read in conjunction with the relevant 1:25,000 ('2½ inch') Ordnance Survey; the entire Stourbridge Canal and much of the Dudley are on sheet SO88/98 (Pathfinder No.933: Stourbridge).

As with previous Towpath Guides, many have contributed to *The Stourbridge Canal* in various ways. I am particularly indebted to Mr Alan T. Smith for pursuing numerous lines of enquiry with characteristic enthusiasm, for assiduously checking the route maps, for providing the greater part of the illustrations and for reading the proofs. I am also grateful to Mr Michael Hale for his interest in the work and for permission to use material from his unrivalled collection of photographs depicting Black Country railways (Plates 26 to 29). His knowledge of the former OW&WR was invaluable in compiling the account of the Stourbridge Extension Canal and the record of Wheeley's basin is largely based on his researches. I am also indebted to Mr Chris Dyche, of the Stourbridge Navigation Trust, for information on the Stourbridge Branch and to the following for providing illustrations: the libraries at Brierley Hill (Plates 4 and 6), Dudley (Plates 2 and 24) and Stourbridge (Plate 23), Mr Peter Freakley (Plate 22), Mr John Greaves Smith (Plate 32) and Mr Arthur E. Truby (Plate 33). Early large scale maps and plans provided the framework around which the route maps, and much of the guide, were devised. For access to these my thanks are due to Mr Basil E. Poole, Johnson Poole & Bloomer, Mr David Hickman of Stourbridge Library and the Department of Geography, The University of Birmingham.

Birmingham   J. Ian Langford
May 1992

1

The Stourbridge Canal

A BRIEF HISTORY

Nowhere does the Staffordshire and Worcestershire Canal pass through the South Staffordshire coalfield and, when the southern section was completed to the river Severn in the spring of 1771, there was clearly a need for a branch to tap the abundant mineral resources in the western part of the coalfield. This region, lying to the west of the ridge which runs through Sedgley and Dudley and traversed by the tortuous outcrop of the famous 10-yard or Thick Coal, along with several other seams and beds of ironstone and fireclay, was not served by the Birmingham Canal, which was then nearing completion. As early as 1662 an Act had been passed for making the river Stour navigable from the Severn to Stourbridge, with a view to tapping these mineral resources. By 1667 this had been carried out by Andrew Yarranton (1616-1681), which was no mean feat; there were numerous mills along the river and the difference in height was considerable. This river navigation was used briefly for the conveyance of coal to Kidderminster and the Severn, but about 1670 the works were evidently destroyed by floods.

Almost a century later the Company of Proprietors of the Stourbridge Navigation was formed, with the intention of constructing a canal from the Staffs & Worcs at Stourton to the town of Stourbridge, a distance of 3¼ miles. The promoters of this scheme included the Earl of Stamford, Thomas Foley and John Hodgetts, through whose land the proposed canal would pass. In February 1766 members of the Company consulted James Brindley, who was then surveying the southern section of the Staffs & Worcs. He surveyed the line and produced a plan of the canal (Plate 1). However, Stourbridge had to wait a further twelve years before it was linked to the canal system.The delay was probably due to caution on the part of the promoters; the success of the scheme depended on the completion of the Staffs & Worcs, which was not opened throughout until 1772. Also, the western limb of the South Staffordshire coalfield was largely unexploited at that time and access to such collieries as existed would have involved lengthy tramways.

All changed when the indefatigable John, 2nd Viscount Dudley & Ward, succeeded to the title and the Dudley estates in 1774. He immediately set about improving communications in the area, with the building of turnpike roads, canals and tramways, and obtained parliamentary powers to enclose vast tracts of Pensnett Chase, with its extensive deposits of coal and other minerals.In 1774 he joined the Stourbridge Navigation Company and was a leading promoter in the revival of the scheme to build a canal from Stourton to the town. A modified line was surveyed by Robert Whitworth (Plate 2), who had assisted Brindley on the Staffs & Worcs, but it was decided at a public meeting held at Stourbridge in February 1775 that there should be a branch to Dudley. A bill for the construction of the canal was submitted to Parliament in the spring of 1775, but there was strenuous opposition from the Birmingham company and from mine owners whose interests would not be served by the canal, and it was withdrawn. Lord Dudley and his fellow promoters, now mainly colliery owners, ironmasters, glassmakers and other local manufacturers, decided to split the proposal, but retain the same line. Accordingly, bills for two separate canals, the Stourbridge and the Dudley, were introduced the following autumn. This time the promoters were successful, despite continuing opposition from the Birmingham company; Acts for the two canals were obtained on 2 April 1776. The Dudley and Stourbridge canals, though built and owned by separate companies, were thus planned as one unit and in many respects were operated as one waterway. Indeed, rarely did the proprietors of neighbouring canals work together in such close harmony, often sharing committee members, officers and employees.

The main line of the Stourbridge (Fig. 1, page 2), as defined in the Act, rises by four locks from its junction with the Staffs & Worcs at Stourton and is then on the level to its terminus near Stourbridge town centre. It crosses the Stour near Wordsley; from here a branch of 2¾ miles rises by 16 locks to the Leys and is then on one level to the Fens on Pensnett Chase, where the Company's reservoirs were constructed. A second branch, from the Leys and 1¼ miles in length, is also on one level and it joins the Dudley at the bottom of Delph locks.Originally there was a 56 yard (51m) tunnel under Brettell Lane, the only one on the Stourbridge system, but this was subsequently opened out. Nowadays, these branches, except for the section to the Fens, are regarded as part of the main line. The Dudley continued up 9 locks (now 8) at the Delph and was then level as far as its terminus at Woodside, a distance of 2¼ miles. The Dudley terminated about 12 feet (3.7m) below the level of the Birmingham and the two canals rose by 267 feet (38.4m) and 29 locks in 7⅜ miles. This heavy lockage made construction both difficult and expensive – the Stourbridge cost about £38,000 and the Dudley £9,700 – and imposed heavy demands on water supplies. The Stourbridge Company was able to construct three reservoirs on Pensnett Chase, the Grove, Middle and Fens pools, but the Dudley was less fortunate. Owing to severe restrictions imposed in the Act, doubtless at the insistence of the Birmingham company, the only site available for a reservoir in the early days of the canal was at Woodside.

The engineer and surveyor for the Dudley was Thomas Dadford who, like Robert Whitworth, had worked under Brindley on the Staffs & Worcs. The equivalent post on the Stourbridge was held by his son, also called Thomas, which provided yet another link between the two companies. The Dadfords were responsible for other Midland canals, but are best known for the considerable mileage of waterways built under their supervision in Wales.

The Dudley was easier to build than the Stourbridge, as it was shorter and there were fewer locks. Work started in 1776 on the 'Level Pond', which followed the contour from Woodside, near the outcrop of the Thick Coal and Lord Dudley's Level colliery. In July 1777 a start was made on Delph locks and construction must have proceeded at a leisurely pace, since the canal was not completed until June 1779. The Stourbridge, with over twice as many locks, three times the mileage and an aqueduct over the Stour, was opened 3 December in the same year.

The Dudley proprietors soon embarked on the building of lengthy tunnels, which was to occupy them for much of the rest of the century, but for the Stourbridge company that was the end, as far as canal construction was concerned. There were proposals to extend the canal to collieries at Shut End* in 1820, but nothing came of them. The lack of action on the part of the canal company to penetrate this developing region at the western extremity of the coalfield in fact prompted Lord Dudley to promote the Shut End (later Kingswinford) Railway to the Staffs & Worcs canal at Ashwood, opened in 1829. A more grandiose scheme emerged in 1836, when a separate company put forward a proposal to link the summit of the Stourbridge with the Birmingham at Bloomfield – the Stourbridge, Wolverhampton & Birmingham Junction Canal. This was strenuously opposed by the Staffs & Worcs and the Birmingham companies, and also by Lord Dudley; in the event only two miles were constructed, from the Stourbridge at Bromley to Oak Farm, a little beyond Shut End. The Act for this canal, known as the Stourbridge Extension, was obtained in June 1837 and it was completed three years later, at a cost of £49,000. Although it was built and operated by a separate company, half the committee members also served on the Stourbridge Committee. Two branches were built, the Bromley (⅜ mile) and the Standhills (³/₄ mile), and the canal was on one level throughout.

From the outset the Extension was of considerable benefit to the Stourbridge, since by that time many mines along the earlier canal were

---

* also Shutt End and Shutend.

largely worked out. In addition to numerous collieries along the Extension, there were several ironworks, six in 1856, including the extensive Corbyn's Hall works. It is small wonder that early railway companies envied the Extension and, after protracted negotiation, it was acquired by the Oxford, Worcester & Wolverhampton Railway in 1847. Indeed, it was one of two important sources of revenue for that company, the other being the Stratford & Moreton Tramway, until the line was opened in the early 1850s. The OW&WR became part of the West Midland Railway in 1860, and this was absorbed by the GWR in 1863.

Throughout the 19th century the Stourbridge was one of the more prosperous canal companies. In addition to being a vital link between an extensive industrial region and the Staffs & Worcs, more than half the total mileage was unaffected by mining activities and the canal was not costly to maintain; subsidence was a continual problem throughout much of the Dudley system and elsewhere in the West Midlands. In the early days of the Stourbridge there was a steady increase in trade and a first dividend on the capital, of about 2½ %, was paid in 1785. This had risen to 14% by 1839/40 and it continued to increase after the opening of the Extension, at a time when many canal companies were beginning to suffer the effects of railway competition. It is hardly surprising that, having absorbed the Dudley, the Birmingham Canal Navigations Co. made an attempt, albeit unsuccessful, to acquire the Stourbridge in 1855. Trade declined during the closing years of the century and in the late 1920s traffic was further affected by competition from road transport, coupled with wholesale closure of collieries throughout the South Staffordshire coalfield. By the time the Stourbridge ceased to exist as an independent company on 1 January 1948, there was little commercial traffic on the canal. A period of decline followed, but the threat of closure and abandonment was averted in the early 1960s. The story of the subsequent restoration of the Stourbridge Canal, leading to the creation of conservation areas along much of it, is related in Chapter 6.

2

The Stourbridge Main Line

BLACK DELPH JUNCTION TO STOURTON JUNCTION

Miles from Black Delph Junction		Miles to Stourton Junction
0 – ¼	Black Delph and Seven Dwellings Bridges	5¼ – 5

The Stourbridge Canal, from its junction with the Dudley at Black Delph Bridge to Leys Junction, follows a winding course around Brierley Hill. The distance by canal is in fact more than twice that by road as it avoids the high ground bounded by the Brierley Hill trough faults, where the productive coal measures are displaced downwards by 100 feet or more. This extra mileage was something of an asset to the company; in addition to the extra tolls payable on through traffic, this section was highly industrialised, as is evident from the remains of numerous wharves and basins along the canal.

Until a few years ago the traveller along the Dudley and Stourbridge canals would have noticed a marked change in the pattern of industry after leaving Delph bottom lock. Here the 'heavy' industry of the Dudley gave way to the characteristic 'beehive' kilns of firebrick works. In the western part of the South Staffordshire Coalfield the seat earth underlying the lower coal seams has a high silica content and is eminently suitable for the manufacture of bricks for furnace and retort linings and other high-temperature applications. The first of these firebrick manufactures, the long-established Delph works (Plate 3), was at the junction, the site being marked by the two roving bridges which spanned the entrance to its basins.

A little further along the canal and on the offside were the wharves and basins of the Brierley Hill District Gas Light Co., whose premises were demolished in 1975. Gas works provided an important source of revenue for canal companies, from the delivery of coal for the retorts and from the shipment of coke and other byproducts of the process. This was particularly true of the Brierley Hill plant, which was not connected to the railway system.

Many brickworks in the area owned their own pits, but others relied on the canal for supplies of fireclay and coal for firing the kilns. The region to the south was honeycombed with workings from several small collieries with interesting names – Louse Park, Delph, Tinker's Field, Turner's Lane, Ashtree, Harding's Field and so on. These were usually connected to the canal by tramways of which two terminated at wharves near Seven Dwellings bridge. During the late 1960s this site was one vast excavation, when 200 feet (61m) of overburden was removed in order to work the Thick Coal. Hereabouts the seam was about 35 feet (11m) in thickness, dwarfing the excavators used to remove it, and numerous 'pillar and stall' workings were exposed. Now the Lakeside housing estate occupies the site. Equipment from one of the Delph pits forms part of the mining display at the Black Country Museum.

⅜   Bowen's Bridge and 'Wheeley's Basin'   4⅜

On the offside near Bowen's bridge are remnants of wharves of the Clattershall firebrick works which survived until the late 1970s. The next bridge carries the Dudley - Stourbridge section of the former OW&WR, opened to traffic in 1852. Immediately beyond, on the towpath side, is the site of the notorious Wheeley's basin which figured prominently in the annals of the Stourbridge Canal.

Industry became established around Brettell Lane, the main Brierley Hill to Stourbridge Road, shortly after the opening of the canal. Initially this amounted to a glass works and pottery close to the outcrop of coal seams and beds of fireclay. The ironworks of Messrs Wheeley Bros soon followed and by the early 1840s there was a double-ended basin here, running parallel to the canal for 170 yards (155m) and extending almost to Brettell Lane. In 1854 this basin was the cause of an altercation between the canal company and the OW&WR. At that time the railway company had no facilities for the transhipment of goods on the canal and an arrangement was made with Wheeley Bros to use their basin. A map produced in 1859, when the ironworks and other Wheeley enterprises were sold by auction, shows the layout of the basin, ironworks and railway (Plate 4). Additional sidings had been constructed at Brettell Lane station earlier in 1854 and goods may well have been conveyed between there and the basin by cart. The canal company threatened to close the basin and take legal action unless this practice ceased. The wrangle continued for a while and eventually the railway company agreed to pay additional tolls on goods carried by canal, but the final outcome was the construction of Bromley interchange basin by the OW&WR on its own canal in 1858/9 (see page 33) and also the interchange facilities at the end of the Stourbridge Branch. A detailed account of this dispute, by T. Foxon, appeared in the March 1989 issue of *Waterways World*.

Roberts and Cooper acquired the ironworks and George King Harrison subsequently built a brickworks alongside part of the basin. This operated until 1975 and was linked by a mineral line to the firm's Nagersfield coal and fireclay mine. To the north of the canal was the chain works of S. Taylor & sons. About 1877 the GWR replaced the long and high timber viaduct across the Coalbourn valley with an embankment and shortly afterwards a spur was built to the brickworks, with a siding along the basin. However, this was a private line to Harrison's works and was not intended for the general transhipment of goods.

On Saturday 14 November 1903, Wheeley's basin was the scene of a spectacular incident; the canal collapsed into mine workings (Plates 5 & 6) , a 'crowner-in', as happened from time to time on the Black Country canal network. Hereabouts the Brooch Coal is a mere 40 feet (12 m) or so from the surface and the Thick Coal is at a depth of 180-200 feet (55-60 m) . The Act for the Stourbridge, in common with other canals in the region, specifically prevented mine owners from working coal under the canal or within 12 yards (11 m) of it, but this was difficult to enforce. Indeed, some 20, 000 tons of Thick Coal alone had to be left to support 100 yards (91 m) of canal and the temptation to ignore the relevant clause was great. Battles over subsidence raged between canal proprietors and mine owners throughout much of the l9th century, but once the coal had been worked there was little the canal companies could do about it, aside from demand compensation or resort to litigation. There were several mines in the vicinity of Wheeley's basin. Harrison's had two fireclay shafts alongside the basin and Harding's Field pit, then mainly worked for fireclay, was on the other side of the railway. The pithead of the old Wheeley's mine was on the side of the Coalbourn valley and across the canal was the abandoned Bretwell Hall colliery. With the whole area riddled with mine workings, subsidence was a continual problem. The fireclay in Harrison's mine, at a depth of 120-150 yards (110-140m) had not been worked for the previous 12 years, since supplies were obtained from the Nagersfield pit (p.14). However, the mine had been kept in working order and in 1902 an exploratory heading in the Brooch coal was driven towards the canal. Although the mine was not developed, this shallow working was probably the cause of the collapse on 14 November in the following year. Ripples appeared on the surface of the canal shortly after 4 o'clock and there was soon a raging torrent as the entire pound from Delph locks to Wide Waters, a distance of almost three miles, emptied itself into a labrynth of old mine workings. Had Jackson's lock, at the start of the Stourbridge Extension, not been closed for the weekend a few minutes earlier, that canal would also have been drained. Two pit frames and a winding-engine boiler fell into the widening cavity and eventually the torrent broke out of the hillside and carved a channel down to the Coalbourn brook. There was no loss of life, since the Saturday shift had just finished, but damage to Wheeley's basin and the adjoining brickworks was considerable. The collapse, was confined to a line parallel to the towpath, between the entrance to the basin and the railway bridge, and to the basin itself, all well within the 'statutory pillar'. Numerous boats were left high and dry, both in the basin and along the main canal (Plates 5 & 6), and the arm nearer the railway bridge was not reinstated.

¾   Long Bridge (Brettell Lane Tunnel)   4½

Long bridge, where Brettell Lane crosses the canal, was formerly a 56 yard (51m) tunnel with a towpath. This was opened out sometime between 1858 and 1880. When the bridge itself was rebuilt a few years ago, the contractors preserved a fragment of the northern end of the tunnel and a part of a side wall at the southern end also survives. The length of the tunnel can be judged by the narrow section.

William Fowler's 1839/40 map of Kingswinford shows Smith's pottery on a site next to the tunnel, but by 1880 it was occupied by a cement works. This no doubt relied on supplies of limestone from Castle and Wren's Nest hills. Next to the cement works and adjoining the towpath was the Brettell Lane colliery, where the Thick Coal is only about 100 feet (30m) below the surface. Here the seam rises rapidly and outcrops 300 yards (274m) to the west, close to the east branch of the Western Boundary Fault. As its name implies, this highly faulted zone is the limit of the exposed part of the South Staffordshire Coalfield. On the offside of the canal, between Long bridge and Bull Street bridge, are the sites of two more firebrick works. The second of these specialised in the manufacture of retorts.

1   Brierley Bridge   4¼

Between Bull Street and Brierley bridges are the long-established premises of the Brierley iron foundry and on the towpath side is the site of the Beanfield pits. The track over the bridge led to the Brierley ironworks, one of the earliest along the Stourbridge. This outpost of the industry centred on Brettell Lane no doubt gave the bridge its name and it closed down towards the end of the 19th century.

The canal curves round the higher ground enclosed by the trough faults and then takes a northerly turn for a short distance. At the bend and on the offside are the remains of a large basin which formerly had three short arms leading from it. Throughout much of the 19th century one of these served Springfield colliery where, owing to the displacement of the trough faults, the Thick Coal was at a depth of 333 feet (101m). Another may have been used by a factory where stone and glass bottles were made. A bank of limekilns, also of early date, was situated alongside the third arm. No trace remains of the roving bridge which gave access to these wharves.

1½	Farmer's Bridge	3¾

The brickworks of Price Pearson occupied a site on the offside beyond Farmer's bridge. This firm was among the last to mine fireclay – in later years it was obtained from opencast workings. The wooden pithead gear, situated alongside the canal, was typical of the small fireclay mines in the area and was dismantled and taken to the Black Country Museum. The company used a former beam winding engine, *ca* 1830/40, to grind the fireclay and this is also stored at the museum.

The crossing of Audnam brook is marked by a large overflow weir, similar to the one on the Level Pond on the Dudley Canal. Opposite were the wharves and basins of a brickworks and an ironworks, marking the start of an industrial region centred on the Leys. Originally these pockets of industry were separated by farmland which may have given rise to the name 'Farmer's bridge', but by the end of the 19th century farming in the region had almost disappeared.

1⅞	Leys Junction and The Leys	3⅜

On the towpath side, as the canal veers westward towards Leys Junction, is the site of Chapman's Field colliery basin, opposite was another ironworks, and beyond the bridge carrying Brierley Hill Road is the Brockmoor iron foundry, formerly the Eagle foundry. To the right at the junction is the Fens Branch (Chapter 4) , now navigable only for a short distance, and to the left is the first of the sixteen locks which take the canal down to the valley of the river Stour.

1⅞	Top Lock (No.1), Stourbridge Sixteen Locks	3⅜

The Stourbridge 'Sixteen' or Wordsley flight descends the spur between the Audnam and Wordsley brooks. The total fall is about 145 feet (44m) and, with an average fall of a little over nine feet (2.7m), the locks are deeper than the majority of those on the BCN. A considerable quantity of water was required to keep commercial traffic moving through the flight and, in addition to the lockage from the Dudley, this was provided by three reservoirs at the end of the Fens Branch. The entire flight is full of interest and is now a Conservation Area.

The top lock has been affected by mining subsidence. This is also true of the entire section between Black Delph and the Leys, but here the result is more obvious. The lock has been raised about 3½ feet (1.1m) and the original sandstone coping can be seen at the lock tail (Plate 7). It was also necessary to rebuild the roving bridge across the tail of the lock and this now has a curious flattened arch. The company's stables, workshop and cottage between the lock and the junction have disappeared.

2⅛	Locks 2 to 4	3⅛

Across the towpath between locks 1 and 2 are two parallel lines of brickwork. These mark the entrance to the basin of Bank's colliery, and a similar basin below lock 3 served the Buckpool colliery. All three locks were damaged by subsidence caused by these pits and the effect on No.3 is particularly severe; here about 5 feet (1.5m) of masonry have been added to the original structure (Plate 8). On the offside below lock 2 was the 'Bottle & Glass' public house which has been re-erected at the Black Country Museum.

At lock 3 the ground begins to fall away more rapidly as the limit of the exposed coalfield is approached and in consequence the locks are now closer together. Along this section the short pounds are enlarged laterally to form extensive reservoirs; otherwise traffic up and down the flight would soon drain the intervening pounds. These side ponds often provided additional wharfage and that above lock 3 had a public wharf alongside Brierley Hill Road. This particular pond in fact extends beyond the road by means of a syphon and the bypass weir is on the opposite side of the road. There was a lock cottage on the offside at lock 4 and the side pond below this lock is larger than usual, owing to the traffic that originated at this point. It has two basins leading from it which were connected to the Nagersfield firebrick works and colliery. Also near lock 4 is the 'Sampson & Lion' public house which formerly had stabling for the 'animals' – horses and mules – of the boatmen. This was a common feature of pubs along rural canals, but the short-haul carriers of the Black country canals normally had their own arrangements for stabling.

2⅜   Locks 5 to 8   2⅞

The eastern branch of the boundary fault crosses the canal between locks 4 and 5 and beyond it the coal seams were too deep to be exploited during much of the 19th century, though occasional attempts were made to do so. A trial shaft about 300 yards (274m) to the north of the canal, known as Bond's Folly, penetrated 840 feet (256m) of the red, stony Enville Beds which occur at the surface between the branches of the fault, but did not reach any coal. A consequence of the fault is that the canal between lock 5 and its terminus at Stourton Junction has not at any time been damaged by mining activities. Aside from the usual repairs and maintenance, this section is basically as it was built 200 years ago. Lock 5 is exceptional, in that it has its original sandstone capping along each side. Erosion by grit-laden towlines normally resulted in the capping being replaced by diamond pattern blue-bricks, as at lock 6. The explanation is probably the high towpath over the roving bridge below the lock. The arch of this bridge is now infilled, but at one time it spanned the entrance to a small basin where coal and limestone for a solitary limekiln were unloaded.

The lock tails throughout the flight have several small differences; there are signs that a cantilever split-bridge spanned the tail of lock 4, lock 6 has a flight of steps on each side and some locks have steps only on one side. The paddle gear is also of interest. This is mostly 'second hand', taken from abandoned sections of the BCN, and the gate paddles attached to sawn off stumps, to serve as ground paddles, look strangely out of place (Plate 10). Most of the old Stourbridge company paddlegear (Plates 14 & 16) has been replaced, but a set has been preserved at the Gloucester Waterways Museum.

Swan Lane crosses the canal at the tail of lock 7. The simple expedient of building bridges across lock tails wherever possible greatly reduced the work involved in constructing bridge approaches. Formerly this was an accommodation bridge carrying the track to the Nagersfield brickworks and colliery and it now gives access to the Hawbush estate. The canal through Buckpool, between Swan Lane and Mill Street, is of exceptional interest. It crosses the western branch of the boundary fault below lock 8 and then traverses Bunter Pebble Beds of Triassic age as far as Bell's Mill bridge. These strata are well exposed in the rock cutting along Brierley Hill Road, a short distance from 'The Swan'. The pounds above and below lock 8 are widened to increase their capacity.

2 ½   Locks 9 and 10: The Staircase (Plates 9 & 10)   2 ¾

The ground falls steeply here due to the same outcrop of Bunter sandstone as can be seen in the road cutting. Thomas Dadford Junior, the engineer in charge of the Stourbridge, evidently overcame this obstacle by building a staircase or double lock, similar to that at Botterham on the Staffs & Worcs Canal. A double lock has a pair of gates which are shared by the upper and lower chambers and thus uses twice as much water as two single locks. As an economy measure the staircase at Buckpool was replaced, probably in the mid 19th century, by two single locks separated by a short pound, an arrangement employed at the Bratch on the Staffs & Worcs. Behind the lock house is a large side pond, known as Jake's pond, which is linked to the pound between locks 9 and 10 by means of a large culvert. Although it is not normally visible, the sandstone responsible for the two locks forms the walls of the culvert. To this day the locks are known as 'The Staircase', despite its having disappeared 150 years or so ago.

A striking feature of 'The Staircase' is the cantilever bridge across the tail of lock 9 (Plate 10), split to facilitate the working of horse drawn boats and grooved by the action of towropes. It has a cast-iron deck and wrought handrails. There were several of these bridges along the Stourbridge and they probably date from 1827, though that at lock 9 could have been re-sited. The steep rise of the canal has preserved the sandstone edging of lock 10 and both locks retain much of their Stourbridge Co. paddle gear.

The lock cottage and outbuildings are in good condition, though the cement rendering does not enhance their appearance, and they form an interesting group. The house has its original hand-made tiles and brick corbels which are characteristic of early 19th century buildings in the area. Surplus water from the pound above lock 9 flows under a wing of the house to Jake's Pond, from which there is an overflow to the tail of lock 10. The old toilet is situated over the bypass channel, as was the usual practice at lock cottages.

Adjoining the towpath is an interesting canalside settlement, The Dock, which fortunately has survived demolition (Plate 11). Formerly this was a group of six cottages, a smithy and stables. It was well established by 1840 and still retains much of its original character. The group includes a general stores and off-license – a source of provisions for families on the working boats and present-day canal users. Next to the shop are gate posts cast at the Brierley Hill ironworks of Hill and Smith.

The side pond below lock 10, unlike others along the flight, is on the same side as the towpath and this departure from normal practice was to enable a dry dock to be constructed alongside lock 11. This basin presumably provided moorings for boats waiting to use the dock, though it may also have been a public wharf.

2 ⅝   Locks 11 and 12: Dock Lock and Shed Lock   2 ⅝

The dock next to lock 11, from which this part of Buckpool gets its name, was constructed in the early days of the canal and went out of use about the end of the 19th century. It was filled with dredgings about 1910 and now only the entrance is visible. The dock, which drained into the pound below lock 11, also served as a bypass for the lock. This arrangement is no longer used and surplus water now flows from the basin above lock 11 to the pound below. Lock 11 has an iron split bridge which formerly gave access to the dock and also to two cottages which were demolished in 1972.

Lock 12 is known as Shed lock, after the wooden transhipment warehouse built by the canal company towards the end of the 19th century (Plate 12). This interesting structure is not rectangular owing to the shape of the restricted site between the lock and its side pond; the shed tapers towards the east, causing the ridge to slope downwards in this direction. Initially the main goods handled here were corn and seeds for the neighbouring Ivy Mills, forerunner of Webbs Seeds, and also hops for a brewery to the north.One side is open to the basin and a canopy, supported by a row of cast-iron columns, extends over the water to protect goods which were being loaded or unloaded. The warehouse was later used by Thomas Bantock, a carrier for the GWR, when it became known as the 'Railway Shed'. There is a coal wharf on the opposite side of the basin and access to Mill Street from both the wharf and the warehouse has stone bollards to protect the brickwork from the hubs of cartwheels. Dadford's Bridge, across the tail of lock 12, is named after Thomas Dadford Junior, who engineered the Stourbridge. This has been widened, but not rebuilt, and the original arch can still be seen.

2 ¾   Glasshouse Bridge (Plate 13)   2 ½

The pound between Dadford's and Glasshouse bridges is dominated by the Red House glassworks of Stuart Crystal, probably founded about 1796. The cone shaped kiln, an ancient monument and now a working museum, is the only complete example of a feature which used to dominate the skyline of Wordsley, Audnam, Brierley Hill and Dudley.

The glass industry was brought to this area early in the 17th century by glassmakers from Lorraine. The region was chosen because of the accessible deposits of coal and fireclay in the neighbourhood. Initially the trade was mainly confined to window glass, bottles and domestic ware, but the manufacture of fine crystal glass became firmly established about the middle of the 18th century. The building of the canal system gave great impetus to the industry; in fact several 'glassmen' were shareholders in the Dudley and Stourbridge companies and served on the committees. In addition to local traffic from the neighbouring coalfield, silver sand was carried by canal from the Leighton Buzzard area on the Grand Union.

Opposite the glass cone is an early roving bridge which spanned the entrance to Joburn's basin. During the latter part of the 19th century this site was occupied by an iron and brass foundry. There were two more glassworks beyond Glasshouse Bridge, White House on the offside and London House alongside the towpath. The former, founded in 1812, is now part of Stuart Crystal.

2 ⅞ – 3 ⅛   Locks 13 to 15 (Plates 14 to 16)   2 ⅜ – 2 ⅛

After No.12 the remaining locks of the 'Sixteen' are wider apart and are separated by normal pounds. There is, however, a slight widening below lock 13 and here the offside bank was strengthened by means of two concrete narrow boats placed end-to-end, but in the winter of 1988/9 one was taken to the Waterways Museum at Gloucester (Plate 14).

The top-gate hanging stones at lock 14 have been replaced and the original massive sandstone blocks can be seen next to the lock. Across the tail is an accommodation bridge of the same design as the roving bridge at lock 1.

3 ¼   Bottom Lock (No.16) and Wordsley Junction   2

The bottom lock is built against a low sandstone cliff near the confluence of Wordsley Brook and the Stour. Owing to the restricted nature of the site, the bypass weir is on the same side as the towpath, whereas at almost all other locks it is on the offside. Wordsley Junction, where the Stourbridge Arm (Chapter 3) branches to the southeast, is immediately below the lock and between the two canals is a colourful outcrop of Bunter sandstone. There used to be a large house at the junction, said to be the residence of the canal manager, and opposite were a cottage and toll office (Plate 17). The roving bridge carrying the towpath of the Stourbridge Branch is mainly original and the narrows are continued to form a gauging stop. Here the freeboard was measured to ascertain the load carried by a boat and hence the toll to be charged. A cavity just above the waterline contained a boom which could be moved across the narrows for gauging purposes or to close the canal at night.

The canal then crosses the river Stour on a two-arch aqueduct which has blue-brick facing and sandstone piers (Plate 18). The river only flows through one arch and, as at the crossing of the Stour by the Staffs & Worcs at Stourton, the second arch was no doubt provided to simplify construction and to carry floodwater. Indeed, when looking at the present narrow and swiftly flowing Stour, it is difficult to imagine that, in the 17th century, the river was navigable between Kidderminster and Stourbridge. The canal enters Staffordshire about 200 yards (180m) beyond the aqueduct and the section between here and Stourton Junction is a conservation area.

| 3 ⅜ – 4 | Bell's Mill and Middle Bridges | 1 ⅜ – 1 ¼ |

The bridge near Bell's Mill and Middle bridge are both original, though they have been repaired and substantially altered. The canal leaves the Bunter Pebble Beds at the first bridge and the next section, through pleasant rural and tree-lined country, is on the slightly older Dune Sands or Lower Mottled Sandstone. This rock is soft and very porous – along the valleys of the Stour and Smestow it is in fact the principal source of drinking water for much of the Black Country – and the strata are inclined downwards towards the river. It is difficult terrain for canal construction and Dadford was evidently aware of the problem, since the vulnerable embankment is protected by massive retaining walls between the towpath and the Stour. Nevertheless, while dredging was in progress during December 1976, the bed of the canal collapsed and the entire pound emptied through a cavity in the underlying sandstone (Plate 19). The scars of the spectacular breach can be seen in the embankment a short distance beyond Bell's Mill, behind the sheet-steel piling.

On the offside are the overgrown mounds of an old quarry, one of several along this section, where the Dune Sands were extracted for use in Black Country foundries and other purposes. Near Middle bridge the canal crosses the boundary of the Upper Mottled Sandstone, which was also quarried extensively, and then leaves the river to take a more southerly course towards Newtown bridge.

4¼   **Newtown Bridge**   1

Although original work is preserved in several bridges along the Stourbridge, by far the best example of a bridge dating from 1776/9 is at Newtown. Structures on the Stourbridge and the Staffs & Worcs have much in common, which is to be expected since only four years separated the canals. The similarity of style is due to the fact that the same contractors worked on the two canals. The coping stones of the bridges are rectangular blocks of Keuper Sandstone and the arches spring from chamfered blocks of the same material, or are of brick. The bridges are otherwise built of red bricks, probably made from local Keuper Marls. A feature of the Stourbridge bridges, rarely found on the Staffs & Worcs, is a stop-plank 'tunnel' in one of the abutments (Plate 17), now mostly sealed with brickwork.

A well-built flight of steps leads from the towpath to the track across Newtown bridge. Its purpose was presumably to provide foot access to the sandpit in the Upper Mottled Sandstone, which extended for about 300 yards (270m) along the towpath.

5 – 5¼   **Stourton Locks**   ¼ – 0

On the offside, as Stourton locks are approached, is a winding hole where sandboats from the numerous pits along this section would turn. The canal then descends by four locks and about 36 feet (11m) to its junction with the Staffs & Worcs. Until recently the upper gate of the top lock was unique, in that it still had a complete set of pre-nationalisation paddle gear – two gate paddles and a ground paddle – and also its original strapping post, stud and other ironwork. The unusually large culvert at this lock is now incorporated as a feature of the neighbouring garden. In fact all the houses on the offside between locks 1 and 2*, built on the site of a couple of small sandpits, have pleasantly landscaped gardens down to the water's edge.

There are a lock cottage and other buildings next to lock 2, where the main Wolverhampton to Kidderminster Road (A449) crosses the canal. Here the towpath crosses to the south side of the canal by means of an iron cantilever split-bridge.

Locks 3 and 4 are closer together and have large side ponds, partly to cope with the substantial traffic which used this section and partly to deal with any sudden rise in the water level. For this reason all Stourton locks have large overflow weirs and there is also a large weir on the Staffs & Worcs, which discharges into the Stour. Immediately above the bottom lock is a basin, an extension of the side pond, which runs

*The locks of the Stourton Flight are sometimes numbered 17 to 20.

parallel to the older canal for almost 100 yards (91m). This was probably used for the delivery and collection of local goods to avoid paying tolls to the Staffs & Worcs, and it may have acted as a 'lay-by' for boats awaiting crews. These arrangements no doubt account for the turnover bridge below lock 2.

| 5 ¼ | Stourton Junction | 0 |

Much of the traffic from the Stourbridge turned south at the junction and for many years there was no building here, loads being gauged at Stewpony on the Staffs & Worcs. About the middle of the 19th century a small toll office was built near the roving bridge and tolls were collected there from northbound boats. The office was in use until nationalisation, but by then there was no toll clerk. The last boats to use this office regularly were those of Thomas Bantock. These carried steel strip and plate from the GWR transit basin at Stourbridge to the Swindon works of Richard Thomas & Baldwin. Tickets were left in a box at the office to be collected each day at 4 o'clock by the toll clerk at Stewpony.

Although Stourton Bridge (No.33) lacks its sandstone coping, the remainder is typical of the early bridges along the Stourbridge, despite the fact that it spanned the Staffs & Worcs; it was of course built by the Stourbridge company as a roving bridge for their towpath. At the junction is a prominent signpost, constructed from old lock beams. This post, installed in February 1977, was the first of several made by members of the Staffordshire & Worcestershire Canal Society and erected at junctions along the waterway.

3

The Stourbridge Branch

STOURBRIDGE WHARF TO WORDSLEY JUNCTION

Miles from Stourbridge Wharf		Miles to Wordsley Junction
0	Stourbridge Wharf	1 ⅜

The main line of the Stourbridge Canal, as authorised in the 1776 Act, ran from the town of Stourbridge to the Staffordshire & Worcestershire Canal at Stourton Junction, with branches from Wordsley Junction to Fens Pool and from the Leys to the Delph, Brierley Hill. However, throughout its working life, the main canal was effectively the section between Stourton and the Dudley Canal at the Delph; the 1⅜ mile length from Wordsley Junction to Stourbridge wharf came to be known as the 'Stourbridge Arm'. Nevertheless, the headquarters of the canal company were at the end of the branch, in offices now used by the Stourbridge Navigation Trust (SNT), and it was an important source of trade, particularly coal to glassworks and other industries throughout its length and goods from the 'railway basin'.

Stourbridge Wharf, at the present terminus of the branch, is dominated by the Bonded Warehouse (Plate 20), a three-storey building with substantial walls up to 18 inches (0.5m) thick and an unusual semi-circular end. Here taxable goods, such as tea, spirits and tobacco, were held 'in bond' until an importer redeemed them by paying the excise duty. The earliest part of the building dates from 1799, twenty years after the opening of the canal, and is thought to have been built on the site of an earlier warehouse. The 1799 structure was probably a single-storey building and by 1829 a second storey had been added. It was extended again in 1849, during the company's most prosperous period, to form the building which exists today. By the mid 19th century a variety of goods were stored there for transhipment, in addition to taxable items. The upper floors extend over the wharf and are supported on a row of cast-iron columns, so that boats could be loaded or unloaded in all weathers. 'Lucams' at the front and rear of the building enclosed hoists which lifted goods from boats or carts to the upper floors. From the early days numerous carriers operated from

Stourbridge Wharf. These included the Shropshire Union Canal Carrying Co., eventually a subsidiary of the L&NWR, and by 1900 the major carrying company of Fellows, Morton & Clayton Ltd, which in 1989 returned to Stourbridge and now operates boat trips along the canal.

In 1980 the warehouse, then vacant and derelict, was designated as a Grade 2 Listed Building. It has since been fully restored, with support from Dudley Metropolitan Borough Council, the former West Midlands County Council, British Waterways Board, the Staffordshire & Worcestershire Canal Society and local residents. The quality and integrity of the work carried out was recognised in 1989 by a commendation in the Civic Trust Awards scheme. The warehouse is now leased by the SNT and rooms are available for use by various clubs and societies and for other functions. There is also a water point and other facilities for boaters at the warehouse.

Across the cobbled Canal Street are the former Canal Company offices (Plate 21), on a strip of land between the street and the river Stour. This interesting building replaced an earlier structure, again in 1849, and is being restored by the SNT. Outside is a weighbridge and adjoining the offices are former cottages which have recently been restored.

In the 1830s the branch was extended for 230 yards (210 m) beyond Lower High Street to serve the Foster & Orme Ironworks. Subsequently the terminal basin (Plate 22) was used by the Stourbridge gasworks for the delivery of coal and for shipping liquid cargoes, probably in the 'tar boats' of Thomas Clayton (Oldbury) Ltd. The short 'tunnel' next to the 'Moorings Tavern' (formerly the 'Barrel Inn') was very low and most cabin boats could not use the basin. In 1859/60 the OW&WR built a 1:14 incline to the basin with a spur along the opposite side of the Stour to Bradley's ironworks. (See below.) The GWR replaced the incline by a steep branchline from Stourbridge Town Station in 1880. All signs of the basin disappeared when the site was developed as the Stourbridge Trading Estate in the mid 1970s.

To the left (south) of the canal and next to the warehouse is Stourbridge Rolling Mills, where various types of rolled steel strip and plate are produced. Curiously, steel was manufactured here, albeit in small quantities, as early as 1835, by one Joseph Young. On the opposite side was the Old Wharf sawmills (Plate 23) which at that time was also owned by Young. Nearby were a bank of limekilns, a standard feature of many public wharves, and the Titan foundry, with its own sandpit in the Dune Sands.

At the end of the wharf area, and the moorings managed by the SNT, are narrows, probably the site of a bridge, where stop planks could be inserted to isolate the final furlong if a breach occurred elsewhere along the branch or main canal. The river Stour follows a winding course along steep-sided valleys as it flows through the western part of the Black Country. Industry was well established along its banks long before the canal era; the power provided by its fast flowing water was used for a variety of purposes, such as the operation of wire and slitting mills, forges or bellows at ironworks. Indeed, the Stour had been made navigable for small craft as far as Stourbridge in the 17th century. It was, however, difficult country for waterway construction and the Stourbridge Branch, at the western limit of the region, is the only Black Country canal to follow the Stour. Its winding route is on sandstone, just above the floodplain of the river, and is mostly bounded by higher ground on the offside. With the risk of a breach ever present, sets of stop planks were kept at bridges and other narrows to isolate a failed section.

⅜   'Bradley's Works' (Plate 24)   1

The towpath starts at the narrows, with access from Canal Street, and there is no public access to the enclosed wharf area. Near the narrows the canal is edged with iron plates and until recently the towpath was surfaced with old puddle-furnace plates. This is the site of a wharf to serve 'Bradley's Works', which occupies the tract of land between the towpath and the Stour. Ash or other waste material was conveyed in barrows along the raised 'pier' here, for loading into boats. John Bradley, a Shropshire man, founded the Stourbridge ironworks in 1798. There were two basins leading into the works. The entrance to the second is spanned by a brick roving bridge which had iron plates along its parapets, but the first and earlier one has an interesting cast-iron bridge. Initially there was no foundry here, since Bradley was primarily a manufacturer of iron bars and hoops, and it was probably for this reason that the bridge was cast at Coalbrookdale. Since the arch castings bear the name of the proprietor as well as that of the manufacturer, it may be that Bradley also had industrial interests in Shropshire. He died a few years after founding the business and his widow married Henry Foster. The works passed to Henry's son, James, who added a foundry to the existing rolling mill and forge, and the Fosters continued to be associated with the Stourbridge Canal throughout the 19th century.

In 1816 James Foster went into partnership with John Urpeth Rastrick and expanded the manufacturing side of the business, specialising in steam engines. It was in fact a union similar to that of

Matthew Boulton and James Watt in Birmingham some years earlier, with Foster providing the business acumen and Rastrick the engineering expertise. Their most famous products were two locomotives made in 1828/29, the 'Agenoria', which Foster operated jointly with Lord Dudley on the Shut End (Kingswinford) Railway (see *A History of the Pensnett Railway*, by W.K.V.Gale and *Towpath Guide No.1*) and the 'Stourbridge Lion', the first locomotive to run on rails in America. In 1885, after a long working life, the 'Agenoria' was given to the Science Museum, London, by William Orme Foster, nephew of James, and the remains of the 'Lion' are in the Smithsonian Institute, Washington.

This, and other enterprises inherited from Bradley, prospered under James's direction and the Fosters, who lived at Stourton Castle, amassed great wealth. However, although James was a leading mine owner and ironmaster in his own right, he continued to trade as John Bradley & Co.. Rolling only ceased in 1982 and to this day the works is known as 'Bradley's'.

The canal turns sharply to the north at the works and here the towpath widens to form another wharf, where recent excavations revealed the base of a crane and the remains of a tramway, with rails set in cobbles, leading into the works. It is likely that the 'Agenoria' started its journey from here, to travel by canal to Ashwood Basin on the Staffs & Worcs, the terminus of the Shut End Railway, and also the 'Lion' and other locomotives, on their way to Liverpool to be shipped to America. Behind the wharf is the elegant, but derelict, Riverside House, once the residence of the works foreman. A curious feature of the house is that the right hand 'windows' on the side facing the canal are painted on the brickwork, possibly to reduce the liability for window tax without destroying the symmetry, so favoured by Georgian builders. Then follows a roving bridge across the narrow entrance to the Company's dry dock, to replace the one at Lock 11 of the 'Sixteen'. This dock, which drained into the Stour, is surrounded by a high wall. Next to the dock and overshadowed by a fine black poplar is a large spillway and a sluice. These were installed so that excess water could pass to the Stour, particularly in abnormal weather, and were part of the arrangements for flood protection along the 3-mile pound between Stourbridge and the top lock at Stourton.

⅞   Coalbournbrook Bridge   ½

Old wharves line the offside as Coalbournbrook bridge is approached, buried under a considerable quantity of tipped material. The wide section here was for the mooring of boats without obstructing the channel and, at the blue-brick wharf, bomb cases were loaded during World War II. There are also steps leading down to a wharf at the northern end of the wide section. Between the towpath and the Stour was the Wollaston edge-tool mill, which existed long before the canal was constructed. The large millpond alongside the towpath disappeared early in the present century and a factory now occupies the site of the mill. Coalbournbrook (Wollaston Road) bridge was widened and strengthened in 1978, buts its original arch was retained. This bridge carried the Kinver Light Railway, which terminated a short distance away at the 'Fish Inn', Amblecote. This tramway, popular in its heyday for outings from the Black Country to Kinver Edge, operated between 1901 and 1930. Beyond the bridge is a well proportioned pumping station, formerly operated by the Stourbridge & District Water Board and now disused, where water was extracted from the Dune Sands. The position of the wharf, where coal for the boilers was unloaded, is indicated by two gate pillars in the towpath wall, near the access ramp from Wollaston Road, and by brickwork in the towpath. Opposite was a winding hole, where the coal boats turned, and at this point the Coalbourn brook enters the canal. This stream is aptly named, since it drains the region between Amblecote and The Delph, where the Thick Coal and other seams were mined extensively. This is the only feed to the Arm, aside from lockage and surface drainage, and a considerable quantity of silt accumulates at this point. Here also was Guest's wharf where six concrete boats were built, by way of a contribution towards saving iron during World War I. Two have survived; these were used as bank protection between lock 13 and 14 of the Stourbridge 'Sixteen' flight (page 18) and one is now preserved in the Waterways Museum at Gloucester.

| 1 ⅛ | Chubb's Bridge | ¼ |

The section through Audnam was lined with industry and wharves. On the offside was a small glassworks, followed the Dial foundry and glassworks adjoining the bridge, where instruments and gauges were manufactured. Opposite is an old sluice paddle enclosed by a fence and then the site of the Audnam iron and brass foundry. The canal crosses the boundary between the Bunter Pebble Beds and the Dune Sands at Chubb's bridge and the latter are exposed in a small cliff on the offside. There were a number of small pits in the Dune Sands hereabouts and these no doubt supplied moulding sand to the Dial works and other foundries along the branch. Chubb's bridge is another original structure though its parapets were damaged by traffic from a former boiler works, successor to the foundry, and have been replaced by galvanised tubing. This bridge, designed to carry nothing heavier than a loaded cart, has in fact survived remarkably well. On the offside beyond the bridge is the glassworks of Tudor Crystal, founded *ca* 1921, which is open to visitors during normal working hours.

A little further along the towpath are Junction Cottages, the remnant of a canal side community, dating from 1829, to which two bungalows have recently been added. Adjoining the first cottage, near where the Audnam brook flows under the canal, is another large overflow weir and a sluice paddle which drain into the brook. The concrete bridge ahead, given the name 'Longboat Lane Bridge', leads to a housing estate built between the canal and the Stour in the late 1970s. The estate is separated from the waterways by a high fence, with no attempt to incorporate the canal and its environs in the overall plan.

1 ⅜   Wordsley Junction   0

At Wordsley Junction the Stourbridge Arm joins the 'Main Line' of the canal. To the right is the Stourbridge 'Sixteen' flight (pages 13 to 19) and to the left is the rural section to Stourton Junction (pages 19 to 21), with a lock-free pound as far as Stourton Top Lock. Owing to the proximity of the bottom lock of the 'Sixteen', the Bunter Sandstone at the junction was cut away to form a low cliff, to make it easier for boats to enter and leave the branch.

* * *

Illustrations

All illustrations are copyright as follows:

AET	Arthur E. Truby
ATS	Alan T. Smith27
BHL	Brierley Hill Library
BWB	British Waterways Board
DL	Dudley Library
JGS	John Greaves Smith
JIL	J. Ian Langford
MH	Michael Hale
PF	Peter Freakley
SL	Stourbridge Library

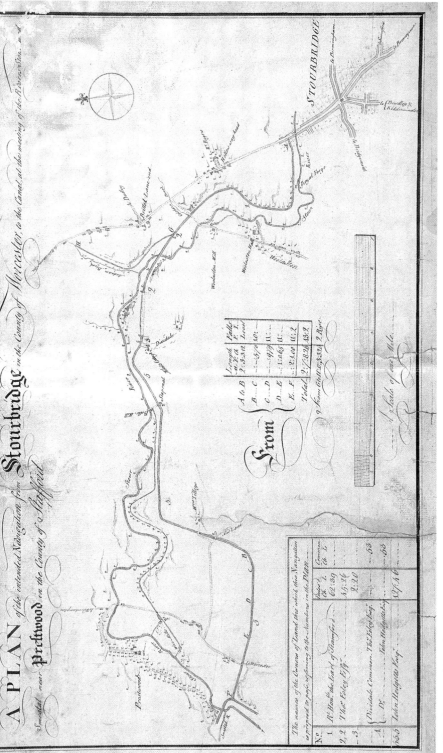

Plate 1: *Proposed line of canal from Stourton to Stourbridge, surveyed by James Brindley early in 1766 when mapping out the southern section of the intended Staffs & Worcs Canal. (ATS)*

Plate 2: *Robert Whitworth's 1774 survey of the Stourbridge Canal, showing the canal as it was eventually built, but with only one reservoir on Pensnett Chase. (DL)*

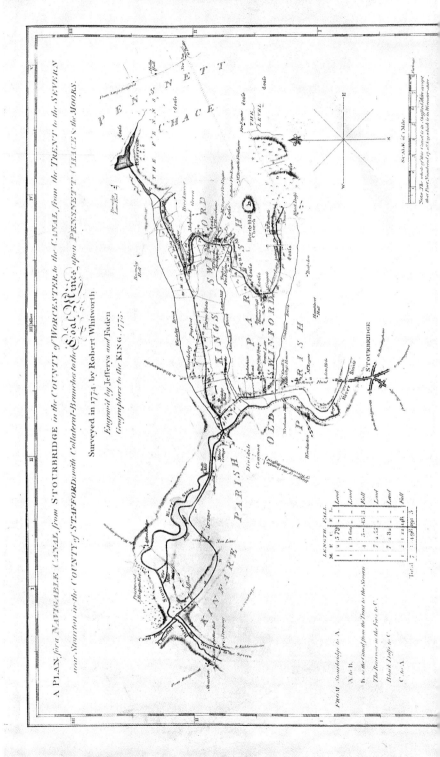

A PLAN for a NAVIGABLE CANAL, from STOURBRIDGE in the COUNTY of WORCESTER, to the CANAL, from the TRENT to the SEVERN near Stourton in the COUNTY of STAFFORD; with Collateral-Branches to the Coal-Mines, upon PENSNETT CHACE & the MOORS.

Surveyed in 1774 by Robert Whitworth

Engraved by Jefferys and Faden
Geographers to the KING. 1775.

Plate 3: *A 'Railway Boat', probably from the former Thomas Bantock fleet, being loaded with refractory bricks in the early 1960s at one of the basins of E.J. & J. Pearson's brickworks at the Delph. (ATS)*

Plate 4: *Part of a plan of the estates of W.S. Wheeley sold by auction on 28 November 1859, showing layout of 'Wheeley's basin', adjacent to the OW&WR, and Brettell Lane tunnel. (BHL)*

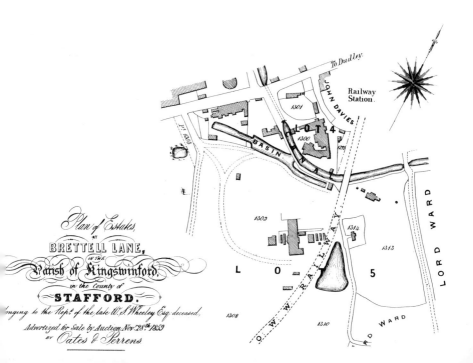

Plate 5: *The 'crowner in' at Wheeley's basin, 14 November 1903; view towards the basin entrance and the George King Harrison's brickworks. Main canal on right and basin on left, where breach occurred. (MH)*

Plate 6: *View of breach from basin entrance, towards railway bridge. (BHL)*

Plates 5 and 6 are from photographs taken four days after the breach occurred.

Plate 7: *Top (No.1) lock of the Stourbridge 'Sixteen' flight, showing extent of mining subsidence at lock tail. (ATS)*

Plate 8: *Effects of mining subsidence at the tail of lock 3.(ATS)*

Plate 9: Locks 9 and 10 ('The Staircase'), with BCN gate paddles on the bottom gates of the latter, and the lock cottage. (ATS)

Plate 10: *Cantilever 'split' bridge at tail of lock 9 and BCN gate paddle used as a ground paddle at lock 10. (ATS)*

Plate 11: *The Dock from lock 11; sidepond alongside towpath, stores and canalside settlement, with 'The Staircase' in the distance. The site of the dry dock is in the right foreground. (ATS)*

Plate 12: *Rear view of timber framed transhipment warehouse adjoining lock 12, formerly used by Thos. Bantock & Co. (April 1992). (ATS)*

Plate 13: *1991 visitor reception area at R House Glassworks (Stuart Crystal) a Glasshouse bridge; remains of old wharf left foreground. (ATS)*

Plate 14: *Pound above lock 13 in 1965, prior to restoration, and SNCo ground and gate paddles. (ATS)*

Plate 15: *Concrete boat used as bank protection on offside below lock 13. (ATS)*

Plate 16: *SNCo ground and gate paddles at lock 15 (October 1975). (ATS)*

Plate 17: *Wordsley Junction ca 1915, with original bridge, gauging stop and company houses, and bottom lock of the 'Sixteen' in the distance. Note cavity in bridge for storing stop planks. (ATS)*

Junction Canal, Wordsley.

Plate 18: *Aqueduct across river Stour under repair in 1992, with 'dry' arch on right. Some surviving original work in piers, but arches mainly of later engineering brick. (ATS)*

Plate 19: *Breach which occurred on 13 December 1976 during dredging operations along embankment at Bell's Mill. (ATS)*

Plate 20: *Restored bonded warehouse at end of Stourbridge Branch, showing lucam and covered wharf.* (ATS)

Plate 21: *Cobbled Canal street, Stourbridge, with bonded warehouse on left and SNCo offices, now the headquarters of Stourbridge Navigation Trust, weighbridge and restored cottages on right. (ATS)*

e 22: Former
& W R / G W R
rchange basin at
of Stourbridge
ch in late 1960s,
tunnel' under
er High Street.
n, subsequently
led and site
eloped. (PF)

Plate 23: *A print ca 1920 depicting the end of the Stourbridge Branch, the sawmill (left) and Bonded Warehouse (right), with Lower High Street in the distance. Curiously, the scene as drawn is reversed. (SL)*

Plate 24: *The Stourbridge ironworks of John Bradley & Co., from Meason's 'Official Illustrated Guide to the Great Western Railway', 1860. (DL)*

THE IRON WORKS OF MR. W. O. FOSTER, STOURBRIDGE.

Plate 25: *Site of Hay Wharf (Brockmoor) bridge, culverted in 1936, in principle the navigable limit of the Fens Branch. (ATS)*

Plate 26: *Stourbridge Extension Canal viewed from Bromley bridge towards the Stourbridge at Brockmoor Junction; Kingswinford Branch of the OW&WR/GWR on the left, Bromley interchange sidings adjoining canal, Jackson's lock with guillotine gates, lock cottage and junction with Bromley Branch (13.10.56). (MH)*

Plate 27: *Transhipment shed at Bromley basin with roving bridge at Brockmoor Junction in the background (27.7.68). (MH)*

Plate 28: *Interior of transhipment shed showing timber frame, possibly as built by the OW&WR, with junction on right (16.6.68). (MH)*

Plate 29: *Stourbridge Extension north of Bromley bridge and Kingswinford Branch of former OW&WR. Bromley Halt has standard GWR pagoda-roofed shelters and in the distance is Bromley brickworks (12.4.55). (MH)*

Plate 30: *'The Crooked House' (Glynne Arms), Himley, ca 1920; a monument to Thick Coal working in the Black Country, in this instance at Oak farm colliery. (JIL)*

ked House Himley Wolverhampton.

Plate 31: *Bridge at Ketley Lane on the Standhills Branch of the Stourbridge Extension, cast by J. Bradley & Co. in 1938. Photograph taken in 1974, prior to its removal to the Black Country Museum for storage. Surviving section of the Branch is to the right of the bridge. (ATS)*

Plate 32: *Artist's impression of 'Bradley's bridge' re-sited across the narrows near the end of the Stourbridge Branch. (JGS)*

Plate 33: *Notices erected at the entrance to the Stourbridge Canal at Stourton Junction. The warning notice on the right appeared early in 1962. (AET)*

Plate 34: *Clearance of lock 9 during the restoration of the 'Sixteen' flight, with the cone of the Red House Glassworks in the background (24.3.67). (JIL)*

Plate 35: *The seal of the Stourbridge Navigation Co., depicting a horse-drawn boat, loaded with coal, in one of the higher locks of the 'Sixteen' flight. In the foreground is a variety of general merchandise, including several barrels. The artist clearly knew little of the working of canals; a towing mast aft of centre would have rendered the boat all but impossible to steer and the unloading of goods while in a lock was strictly prohibited! The seal has some similarity with that of the Dudley Company, since both depict a lock and a pumping engine belching forth black smoke. A severe storm completes the scene, though the rainbow is perhaps symbolic of better times ahead. (BWB)*

4

The Fens Branch

LEYS JUNCTION TO BROCKMOOR BASIN

Miles from Leys Junction		Miles to Brockmoor Basin
0 – ¼	Leys Junction to Brockmoor Junction	⅞ – ⅝

What is now known as the Fens Branch, together with the 'Sixteen' flight, formed one of the two collateral cuts mentioned in the 1776 Act. The other, now part of the main line, heads eastwards at Leys Junction, towards the Dudley at Delph locks. The Fens Branch and the 'Sixteen' were opened at the same time as the former main line to Stourbridge and the branch was effectively a navigable feeder, supplying water to the rest of the Stourbridge system. However, it was also an important source of trade, as is evident from traces of basins, roving bridges and wharves throughout its length. In the angle between the branch and the present main line at the Leys was the Eagle iron foundry, followed by a brick and tile works on the offside, with coke ovens adjoining the towpath. Now modern industrial units flank the canal as far as Brockmoor Junction.

¼	Brockmoor Junction	⅝

At Brockmoor is the junction with the Stourbridge Extension Canal (Chapter 5). Near the junction was another foundry and an iron and tinplate works which later became part of the Cookley Works of Richard Thomas & Baldwin. The towpath of the Fens Branch crosses the Extension by a riveted iron roving bridge of typical GWR design.

¼ – ⅝	Brockmoor Junction to Hay Wharf (Brockmoor) Bridge	⅝ – ¼

Brockmoor Junction is effectively the limit of navigation; in principle the culverted Hay Wharf bridge prevents boats from reaching the end of the Fens Branch, but the section after the junction is badly silted and nearly derelict. Adjoining the junction is the bridge carrying the Kingswinford Branch of the former OW&WR, opened to Oak Farm in 1860. Work by the GWR on extending the line to Oxley, near Wolverhampton, started in 1913, but was interrupted by the First World War and it was not ready for use until January 1925.

To the west, between the railway and Haywood bridge, is the deep valley of the upper reaches of Wordsley brook, accentuated by subsidence. Looking back there is a view of the impressive embankment of Bromley basin and the start of the Extension Canal. Until recently, Haywood bridge, which carried Cresset Lane, was a precarious structure, much affected by subsidence and with signs of having been repaired frequently. It has now been rebuilt and the lane has been reduced to a public walkway. The sportsfield beyond the bridge occupies the site of the Bromley colliery and ironworks and the small basin on the offside was at the end of a tramway from a pithead of the Wallows colliery. In August 1935 the Stourbridge Company obtained an Act of Parliament, mainly to change tolls and other charges levied, but also to abandon Brockmoor basin at the end of the Fens Branch. A clause in the Act authorised the transfer of Hay Wharf bridge, also known as Brockmoor bridge, to Staffordshire County Council.

$\frac{5}{8} - \frac{7}{8}$ **Wide Waters and Fens Pools** $\frac{1}{4} - 0$

The Fens Branch terminates in the long and broad Brockmoor basin, known as 'Wide Waters'. The towpath crosses to the east side of the canal at Brockmoor bridge and behind the embankment on the offside is Grove Pool, the first of the three reservoirs which supply the Stourbridge canal. The whole area was mined extensively - the Thick Coal was only about 500 feet (152 m) below the surface - and much of the terminal basin was flanked by coal wharves. Those at the head of the canal had sidings from the Pensnett Railway, which linked the Earl of Dudley's collieries, ironworks and other enterprises in the region, from Baggeridge to Cradley. These wharves were a major source of coal traffic throughout much of the life of the canal, particularly after the original narrow-gauge system was converted to standard gauge in 1869.

Grove Pool was built at the same time as the canal, but it immediately became apparent that this could not adequately meet the needs of the 'Sixteen'. The supply was increased a year later by the provision of two more reservoirs, Middle Pool and Fens Pool. All three reservoirs were connected by an elaborate system of brick culverts and weirs. These have been replaced in recent years, but traces of the original works can still be seen. There were continual problems from subsidence; Middle Pool had all but disappeared by the 1880s and was not reinstated until the mines closed and pumping ceased. The whole area surrounding the reservoirs and Wide Waters has been attractively landscaped; spoil heaps have been graded, trees planted and paths created along the trackbed of various ramifications of the Pensnett Railway, to create a valuable amenity for local residents.

5

The Stourbridge Extension Canal

Built during the late 1830s and opened in 1840, the 2-mile Stourbridge Extension is the only canal covered in this guide which dates from the dawn of the railway era. It penetrated a region rich in accessible deposits of coal, ironstone, fireclay and marl, where industry was well established. In 1840 there were already three ironworks along its line - the Leys (or Lays), Corbyn's Hall and Foster's Shut End works, which traded as 'J. Bradley & Co.' - and there were a couple of dozen or so mines within a few hundred yards of the canal. Although there was some competition from the Shut End Railway (p.7), the Extension was a profitable venture from the start, but its heyday was short-lived; the arrival of the Kingswinford Branch of the OW&WR in 1860 heralded the onset of a steady decline in traffic. Today a mere 200 yards (183 m) is still navigable and this section is known as Bromley Basin.

Along the offside of the basin were sidings from the Kingswinford Branch of the OW&WR, for the interchange of goods between the railway and the canal (Plate 26). These were opened late 1858 or early 1859, when construction of the line from Kingswinford Junction had reached Bromley. The siding adjoining the canal terminated in a substantial wooden-framed shed, later clad in corrugated iron, which overhung the basin for the transhipment of goods requiring protection from the weather (Plates 27 & 28). The opening of the interchange basin clearly diverted some traffic from the Stourbridge, but this was offset by short-haul traffic from that canal to Bromley basin, particularly in later years.

At a short distance from the junction, on the towpath side, was the entrance to a long basin running parallel to the Stourbridge for 230 yards (210 m). This basin, linked by tramways to the Leys ironworks, was for the conveyance of goods and raw materials to or from the Extension without incurring tolls on the Stourbridge and was constructed in the early 1840s. Bromley basin, the interchange sidings and the Kingswinford line share a high embankment across the valley of the Wordsley Brook and at the end of this is the infilled Jackson's stop lock. Mine owners wishing to use the canal were obliged to pump water into it, but otherwise there were no water supplies and an elaborate double lock for measuring water flowing to or from the Extension was a requirement of the 1837 Act. The intention was for the company with the higher water level to levy a charge for lockage, provided that the difference in levels exceeded 6 inches (15 cm). Soon after the opening of the canal it was realised that this arrangement was unworkable and the 132-foot (40 m) lock was thereafter only used for gauging purposes and for closing the canal at weekends. The Fens Branch of the Stourbridge and the Extension were thus effectively on one level, but as recently as 1936 there was a dispute between the Stourbridge Company and the GWR over the loss of water into old mine workings along the line of the Extension. At a time when traffic had all but disappeared from the rest of the Extension and much of it had been closed, a guillotine lock was installed in August 1937. The 1935 SNCo Act in fact included provision for the transfer to the Stourbridge Company of what remained of the extension, but this had clearly not been implemented at that time. The steel uprights for the guillotine gates were removed about 1970, when the sidings were lifted and the transhipment shed was demolished. Adjoining the lock were a cottage and the canal's only toll office, followed by a brick roving bridge at the junction with the Bromley Branch (Plate 26).

Aside from Bromley basin, little remains of the Extension and its branches. Indeed, few canals have been so effectively obliterated. The section beyond Bromley bridge survived until the 1960s (Plate 29), but a housing estate was built on it during the late 1980s and the rest of the Extension largely disappeared when the Pensnett Trading Estate was developed. All that remains to mark the line of the canal are a few fragments of old hedgerow or traces of embankment. However, the site of the terminal basin, now occupied by a brickworks, can be identified at a bend in Oak Road. This is about 600 yards (550 m) to the southeast of the 'Crooked House' (formerly the 'Glynne Arms') (Plate 30), a pub which has capitalised on the extreme effects of subsidence caused by working the Thick Coal and other seams at Oak Farm colliery. The Extension and its branches were on one level throughout, which necessitated the construction of several embankments and the one at the terminal basin is a particularly impressive example. This particular embankment, which is faced with blast-furnace slag, was needed to bring the canal as near as possible to collieries and brickworks around Oak Farm.

THE STOURBRIDGE EXTENSION CANAL

The Bromley Branch

The Extension's two branches were constructed to tap the western extremity of the exposed coalfield, beyond which the productive measures plunge to a depth of some 1500 feet (460 m) or more and were thus inaccessible throughout much of the 19th century. Nevertheless, there was intensive mining activity right up to the Western Boundary Fault; here the Thick Coal is only about 500 feet (150 m) below the surface, though mining was somewhat unpredictable in this faulted 'broken' ground and the life span of individual mines was relatively short.

The shorter (⅜)-mile Bromley Branch was opened a year or so after the main canal. There were a number of collieries along or near the branch – Slater's Hall, Crab Lane, Little Meadow and Coal Leasows, plus a number of small pits whose records have not survived. All had closed by 1882 and by then much of the branch had been drained, but Coal Leasows was reworked during the first 20 years or so of the present century and the branch was reinstated. The end of the Bromley Branch was about 250 yards (230 m) from the boundary fault and 450 yards (410 m) to the southeast of 'Bond's Folly' (page 15).

The Bromley branch, though infilled, can be traced in its entirety and, from the site of its only bridge at 200 yards (180 m) from the main canal, an ash path follows its line. This is part of a network of tracks which traverse the site of Coal Leasows colliery, now landscaped, with links to the Fens Branch and the top lock of the 'Sixteen' flight.

The Standhills Branch

The ¾ mile Standhills Branch left the main canal about ½ mile from the stop lock and terminated a mere 100 yards (90 m) from the Western Boundary Fault. It was opened towards the end of 1840 and at that time there was no industry whatever throughout its length. Its main purpose was to carry coal and other minerals from this unexploited region, but it was also intended to generate local traffic, since wharves and limekilns were provided at the terminal basin on the western side of Ketley Road (formerly Green Lane). A winding, banked track, about ½ mile in length, was also constructed from the end of the canal to Halfway, on the road between Kingswinford and Stourbridge, which was no doubt used for the conveyance of goods by cart. Part of this track survives as an access road to the rear of houses in The Portway, Kingswinford. Whatever the arrangements were for general wharfage, they can only have been operative for a few years; the spoil from the neighbouring

Horton colliery, on the line of the boundary fault, soon engulfed the area around the terminal wharves. By the end of the 19th century the branch beyond Ketley Road had been drained.

Other collieries along the branch were Standhills and, near the terminus, Ketley. All three had closed by 1880, though Standhills was reopened briefly during World War II. By this time the branch was no longer navigable – indeed, spoil from the mine had obliterated part of it – and coal was taken away by means of a siding, along the line of the canal, to the Kingswinford Railway. Another source of trade on the branch was Ketley Quarry. Here, as along much of the main canal, Old Hill (Etruria) Marl occurs at the surface, and this is used extensively for the manufacture of bricks, tiles and related products. Ketley quarry expanded considerably in the 1930s and engulfed some 200 yards (180 m) of canal towards the end of the branch. The 19th century brickworks was demolished to give access to further deposits of marl and the clay is now transported by lorry to the brick and tile works of Hinton, Perry & Davenhill in Dreadnought Road, Tansey Green.

An interesting iron bridge was constructed where the lane to Ketley house (now demolished) crossed the Standhills Branch. This was cast by J. Bradley & Co. and it bears the date 'AD 1838' (Plate 31), indicating that the branch was constructed at the same time as the main canal. The bridge was removed to the Black Country Museum in 1974, when the neighbouring sportsfield was extended. Currently there is a proposal to erect it near the end of the Stourbridge Arm (Plate 32), a short distance from the foundry where it may have been cast over 150 years ago. However, it is more likely to have been produced at Bradley's Shut End ironworks and shipped the 1½ miles to Standhills by canal. From the site of the bridge, near the southern end of Ketley Road, is the only surviving length of the Stourbridge Extension, aside from Bromley basin. This 250-yard (230 m) length, severed by Ketley quarry, starts in a shallow cutting and then has a low embankment and, though drained, is in a remarkably good state of preservation. The sides are lined with thick brick walls, as they were along much of the main canal, and clearly display the high standard of construction employed on the Stourbridge Extension.

Decline and closure of the Stourbridge Extension Canal

Various factors brought about the decline, closure and eventual annihilation of the Extension. The basic cause, aside from the fact that it should have been built as part of the Stourbridge some decades earlier, was the lack of a through route and its prosperity thus depended solely on trade generated along its line. A main purpose of the Extension was to carry coal – in 1905, for example, this accounted for 80% of the tonnage carried – and other minerals, and its fortunes followed those of the mining industry. By the 1880s, the majority of the innumerable mines along or near the canal had been worked out and abandoned and in 1909 only those at Oak Farm (Himley Firebrick Co), Shut End (J. Bradley & Co) and Corbyns Hall (Stourbridge Glazed Brick & Tile Co) were operative.

Another consideration is the decline of the iron industry towards the end of the l9th century. In 1873 there were 15 blast furnaces along the canal, though even then many were not in use, and by the end of the century most had gone, as had the scores of puddling furnaces and the numerous mills and forges; only Corbyn's Hall New Works appears to have changed to steel making. The only industry which expanded, and which thrives to this day, is the manufacture of bricks and other clay products, but this did not use the canal to any great extent in later years.

A significant factor in the decline of the Extension was ownership by the GWR, a company which did little to encourage trade upon its canals, particularly when a railway ran alongside, as was the case with the Extension. However, the canal was tolerated, since it was the only waterway owned by that company which made a profit, albeit a modest one (£689 in 1905 for example). Also, maintenance costs were normally not high; there was an adequate depth of water due to mining subsidence and no dredging was necessary, or so the company claimed, but occasionally the cost of repairing subsidence damage resulted in a trading loss. However, tolls on the canal were high, since there were no concessionary charges for through traffic, as was required on other canals under the Provisional Order Act of 1894. This had the effect of diverting trade to the many sidings from the Kingswinford railway which had been constructed to several major industries along the Extension by the latter part of the l9th century. Also, aside from economic considerations, there was little point in conveying goods by canal to Bromley interchange basin when they could be loaded directly into wagons at source.

By the 1920s relatively few boats travelled the full length of the canal and the GWR began to close it, a section at a time, starting with the remainder of the Standhills branch in 1928. The main line was reduced in stages during the 1930s and by 1937 it was only open as far as Lenches bridge. This length was later severed by the construction of the siding to the re-opened Standhills colliery and was finally abandoned as far as the stop lock in 1960. From the 1950s onwards the vast acreage of derelict land traversed by much of the Extension, formerly the scene of intensive industrial activity, was redeveloped as the Pensnett Trading

Estate. However, much of the original Kingswinford Branch of the OW&WR survives to this day, effectively as a long siding from Kingswinford Junction to the Pensnett coal concentration depot, on the site of former sidings to Bradley's Shut End works. This was opened in 1964 by Messrs Lunt, Comley & Pitt, as part of their development of the trading estate, and coal is still delivered by rail. There is a fascinating account of the Kingswinford Branch and its numerous siding, with many anecdotal references from those who worked on the railway during the present century, in *The Railway to Wombourn* by Ned Williams (Uralia Press – Wolverhampton, 1986).

6

Restoration and Conservation

Thirty years ago the entire Stourbridge Canal was threatened with extinction, but the present main line is now part of the 'Cruiseway' network, two thirds form linear Conservation Areas and a mere ½ mile is no longer navigable. Its remarkable story during the past three decades may not be unique, but the extensive cruising network which exists today owes much to the precedent created by the restoration of the Stourbridge.

On 1 January 1948 ownership of most canals and river navigations passed to the British Transport Commission (BTC), along with railways, docks and road haulage. By that time there were few carriers left on the Stourbridge, though the last struggled on until the early 1960s. Little maintenance was carried out, decay and dereliction set in and there was a danger that this important link between the Black Country system and the Staffs & Worcs Canal would be lost for ever. These were the days of wholesale abandonment - or attempted closure - of canals, but there were also vigorous campaigns to keep them open. Matters came to a head at Stourbridge in 1961 when the BTC announced its intention to include the Stourbridge as a candidate for closure, along with twelve other canals, in a bill to be considered by Parliament the following year. Alarmed by this proposal, members of the Staffordshire & Worcestershire Canal Society (S&WCS) attempted to cruise to Stourbridge, in order to draw attention to the plight of the canal. However, by this time the canal had deteriorated to the point of being barely navigable and the procession ground to a halt ½ mile from the town. This was not entirely due to lack of maintenance; the early 1960s saw the spread of vandalism throughout the land and the semi-derelict canal system was particularly vulnerable; bridge parapets, locks and empty canalside property were all targets for this new-found pastime and the Stourbridge Branch did not escape the attention of the youth of the day. Offers were made to clear the canal voluntarily, but the BTC refused to co-operate, neither with the Society, nor with the Inland Waterways Association (IWA), whose annual rally was to be held at the end of the Stourbridge Branch in August 1962. Much of the

Stourbridge was then within Amblecote Urban District and the Council supported the BTC proposal. The Planning Committee was unanimous in wanting the canal infilled, since 'it had outlived its usefulness'. Brierley Hill Council, on the other hand, through whose district the upper part of the canal passed, took a more enlighted view and strongly supported its retention for leisure purposes.

In February 1962, 'warning' notices appeared at the top of the 'Sixteen' and at Stourton Junction, stating that the flight was 'unsuitable for the passage of vessels', which should not 'attempt to navigate through the locks' (Plate 33). Furthermore, the BTC steadfastly refused to clear the Stourbridge Arm, or carry out any work on the locks, and continued to prevent volunteers from doing so. As boats began to converge on Stourbridge during the summer months, it became clear that drastic action was needed, otherwise few would reach the rally site. On 25 July a dragline mysteriously appeared on the Stourbridge Branch, quickly followed by two local BTC officers, who threatened legal action if the dragline's bucket so much as created a ripple. David Hutchings, chairman of the Midland Branch of the IWA, gave orders for work to proceed. A further threat of litigation was issued, this time from the BTC South-Western Division manager at Gloucester, whereupon the IWA sought legal advice and decided to carry on with the dredging. In the meantime the 'Battle for the Stourbridge' was receiving widespread publicity, both locally and nationally, highlighting the intransigence of the BTC. The Member of Parliament for Brierley Hill, John Talbot, even visited the site and tabled a motion in the House of Commons 'to let private enterprise carry out repairs to canals which the nationalised canal system refuse to undertake'. In the face of this adverse and embarrassing publicity, the BTC capitulated on 28 July; an announcement from the headquarters in London gave permission for dredging to continue and on 30 July a full length boat, loaded with rubbish from the canal, reached the end of the Stourbridge Arm.

1962 was the turning point in the fortunes of the Stourbridge. The rally, held 13/18 August, was a great success, in that it was attended by 118 boats, several having forced their way down the 'Sixteen'. However, of more importance was a stay of execution for the Stourbridge and other canals, as a result of the intensive publicity. Also, a positive feature of the Transport Act of September 1962 was the decision to transfer ownership and management of the nationalised waterway system to an independent Board, responsible directly to the Minister of Transport. Thus, on 1 January 1963, British Waterways Board (BWB) was created.

The new custodians of the canals and navigable rivers, aware of the potential for cruising and other leisure activities, which were increasing in popularity at the time, soon developed a more enlighted attitude towards their charge. Also, in so far as many canal 'enthusiasts' were concerned, confrontation gave way to collaboration; in June 1963 the S&WCS held a small rally at the Stourton village fete and, in preparation for this, the Society was allowed to do limited remedial work on the four locks at Stourton. This was probably the first time that a voluntary body had been permitted to carry out such work on a canal. Later in the same year two members of the Board visited the Stourbridge with officers of the Society to inspect the canal and consider its future. In a statement made by BWB shortly afterwards, the Staffs & Worcs was to be retained for pleasure purposes, but the fate of the Stourbridge would depend on 'local interest'. Of this there was an abundance; further discussions were held, which resulted in the decision to restore the 'Sixteen' flight. Work started soon afterwards and was completed in 1967.

The restoration of the locks was a milestone in the annals of the canal system. For the first time volunteers and BWB employees worked side by side in a major restoration project, a precedent which paved the way for similar schemes throughout the country. Nine top gates and five sets of bottom gates had to be replaced and volunteers helped to install over half of these and assisted in repairing the gates which were retained. The most important task undertaken by members of the S&WCS and other volunteers was the clearing out of lock chambers (Plate 34); often silt and refuse had accumulated to a depth of 3 feet or more. Towpath walls also were rebuilt and repairs were carried out to lock chambers, wing walls, weirs and culverts. This remarkably successful co-operative venture culminated in the re-opening of the Main Line of the Stourbridge on 27 May 1967 by John Morris, MP, the Parliamentary Secretary to the Minister of Transport. The opening ceremony took place at lock 11 and was followed by a cruise to Stourton Junction.

In the following year, under the provisions of the 1968 Transport Act, the future of much of the canal system was assured with the creation of 'Cruiseways'. These canals, which include the Main Line of the Stourbridge, are maintained to a fully navigable standard. Others, such as the Stourbridge Arm, were classified as 'Remainder Waterways'; for these the Board's statutory obligations are only concerned with maintaining a water channel and with matters of public health and safety. However, some canals in this category have subsequently been upgraded to 'Cruiseways'. Another event with far reaching consequences for the waterway system was the passing of the Civic Amenities Act in 1974. This provided for the creation of 'Conservation Areas', with strict local-authority control over all forms of development within their bounds, and for the protection of buildings having particular architectural or historic merit. By 1980 the Main Line from the top of the 'Sixteen' to Stourton Junction had been given Conservation-Area status and the canal's environs have been greatly enhanced as a result. Unfortunately, the provisions of the Act did not include the canal itself; its character has to some extent been impaired by unsympathetic maintenance and remedial work and several features from pre-nationalisation days have been lost.

Although the Main Line flourished, following its re-opening in 1967, the Stourbridge Branch continued to deteriorate and in 1972 the S&WCS produced a report drawing attention to its condition. Among the recommendations made was the creation of a marina between Coalbournbrook and the dry dock, with infilling of the end of the Arm for an access road and redevelopment. Also, from 1973 onwards the Society organised a series of working parties to clear as much of the channel as was practicable with voluntary effort. Then, in the late 1970s, the West Midland County Council, which had been created on 1 April 1974, dredged the entire arm, re-surfaced the towpath and improved the canal's environs, as part of land reclamation work in the area. The Bonded Warehouse was designated a Listed Building on 24 April 1980 and on 17 June 1986 the 'Sixteen' Conservation Area was extended to include the Stourbridge Branch. The warehouse has since been restored and is used for a variety of purposes by the local community, secure moorings have been created at the end of the branch and the former company offices are being restored. Amblecote UDC has long since disappeared, as has the BTC, but the Stourbridge Arm has survived and is a well maintained waterway, 'Cruiseway' in standard, if not by designation. The branch is now a valuable amenity for local residents and visitors alike; the vision of those who opposed its closure thirty years ago has been amply justified.

7

Route Maps

'Main Line' of the Stourbridge Canal   Maps 1–6

Stourbridge Branch   Map 7

Fens Branch   Map 8

Stourbridge Extension Canal   Map 9

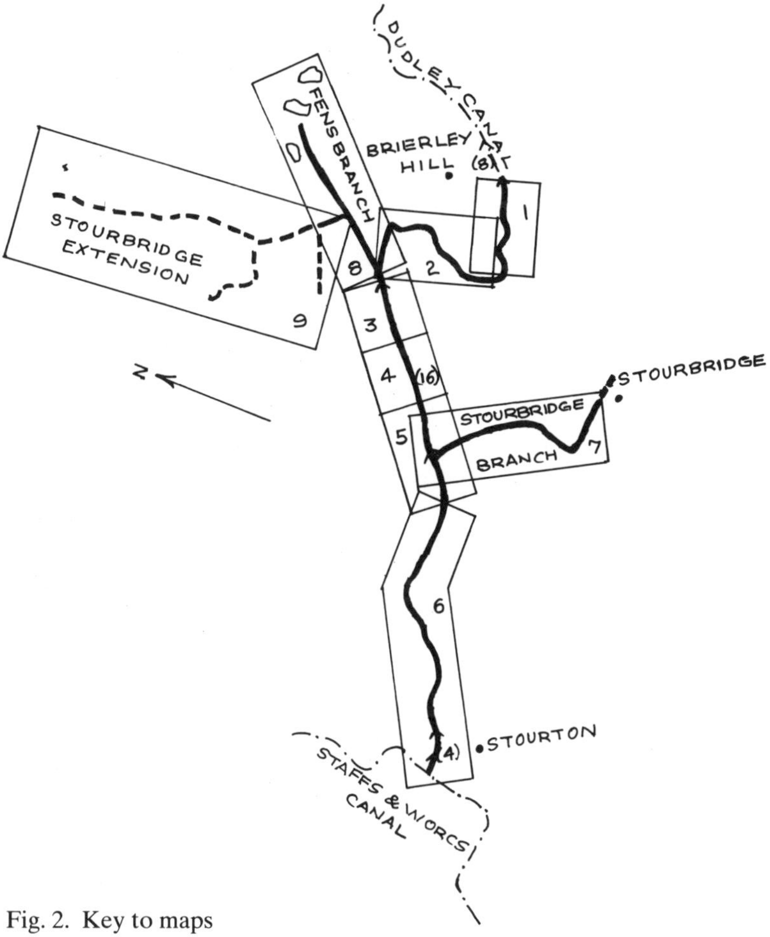

Fig. 2. Key to maps

43

Stourbridge Main Line

MILES FROM
DELPH J.

'TENTH
LOCK'

THE VINE ¼ ML.
[BATHAM'S HOME-
BREWED ALE]

MILES TO
STOURTON J.

DELPH BOTTOM
LOCK: No. 8 (9)
8'6" FALL

HOVEL

1858 [R;CD;W]
WEIR

THE DELPH

BRIERLEY HILL

'THE BELL'

DELPH   BRIDGE

0   DELPH JUNCTION

BCN

DUDLEY C? (BCN)
—— BOUNDARY —·—·—
STOURBRIDGE C?

5¼

(PRE 1840 BASIN)

(DELPH FIREBRICK

WORKS) DEM. 1975

WITHYMOOR ESTATE

(PRE 1840 BASIN)

WH

(BRIERLEY HILL
DIST. GAS C?
DEM. 1975

WHARVES

WHARF

+ + + +(DELPH COLLIERY)

(SL)

(AND   FIRECLAY)

CONCRETE
WORKS

356'

NEW WORKS BR.

⊕ (LOUSE PARK COLLIERY
No. 4 PIT: 180' TO THICK COAL)

¼

SEVEN DWELLINGS BR.

5

SILVER END

(GLASS
BOTTLE
WORKS)

WHARF

+ + + + (CROWN PITS AND WORKS)

⊕ (LOUSE PARK COLLIERY
No. 3 PIT: 187' TO THICK COAL)

(CLATTERSHALL
FIREBRICK
WORKS)

WEIR

+ +

FIRECLAY

+ +

PITS

+ +

(COAL   FOR

(W'TON)

O.W. & W.R.

(BRETTELL LANE STA.)

+ +
+ +
+ +

BOWEN'S BRIDGE

+ +

⊕(HARDING'S FIELD
COLLIERY: 181' TO THICK COAL

(OPENCAST

5/8

(BRETTELL LANE
GLASS HOUSES,
LATER CHAIN WORKS)

STOURBRIDGE J.

4⅝

(PRE 1840 BASIN)
('WHEELEY'S')

(GEORGE KING
HARRISON: BRETTELL
LANE FIREBRICK WORKS)
DEM. 1975

DELPH ROAD

44

②

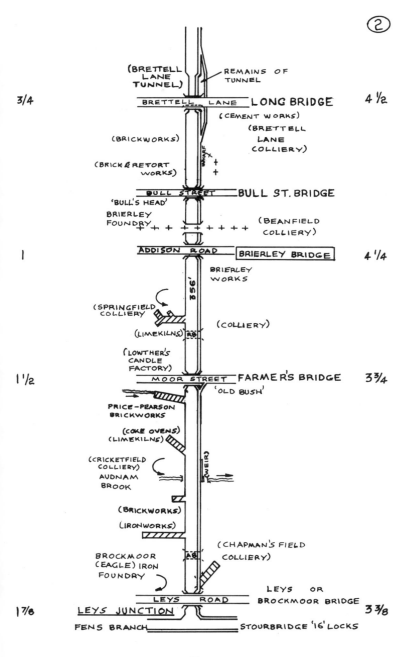

(BRETTELL LANE TUNNEL)   REMAINS OF TUNNEL

3/4

BRETTELL LANE   LONG BRIDGE   4½

(CEMENT WORKS)

(BRICKWORKS)   (BRETTELL LANE COLLIERY)

(BRICK & RETORT WORKS)

WHARF
×
+
+

BULL STREET   BULL ST. BRIDGE

'BULL'S HEAD'
BRIERLEY FOUNDRY   (BEANFIELD COLLIERY)
+ + + + + + + +

ADDISON ROAD   BRIERLEY BRIDGE   4¼

1

BRIERLEY WORKS

356'

(SPRINGFIELD COLLIERY)

(LIMEKILNS)   (COLLIERY)

('LOWTHER'S CANDLE FACTORY)

1½   MOOR STREET   FARMER'S BRIDGE   3¾

'OLD BUSH'

PRICE-PEARSON BRICKWORKS

(COKE OVENS)
(LIMEKILNS)

(CRICKETFIELD COLLIERY)
AUDNAM BROOK

(WEIR)

(BRICKWORKS)

(IRONWORKS)

(CHAPMAN'S FIELD COLLIERY)

BROCKMOOR (EAGLE) IRON FOUNDRY

A8

LEYS   OR   BROCKMOOR BRIDGE

LEYS ROAD

1⅞   LEYS JUNCTION   3⅜

FENS BRANCH _____   STOURBRIDGE '16' LOCKS

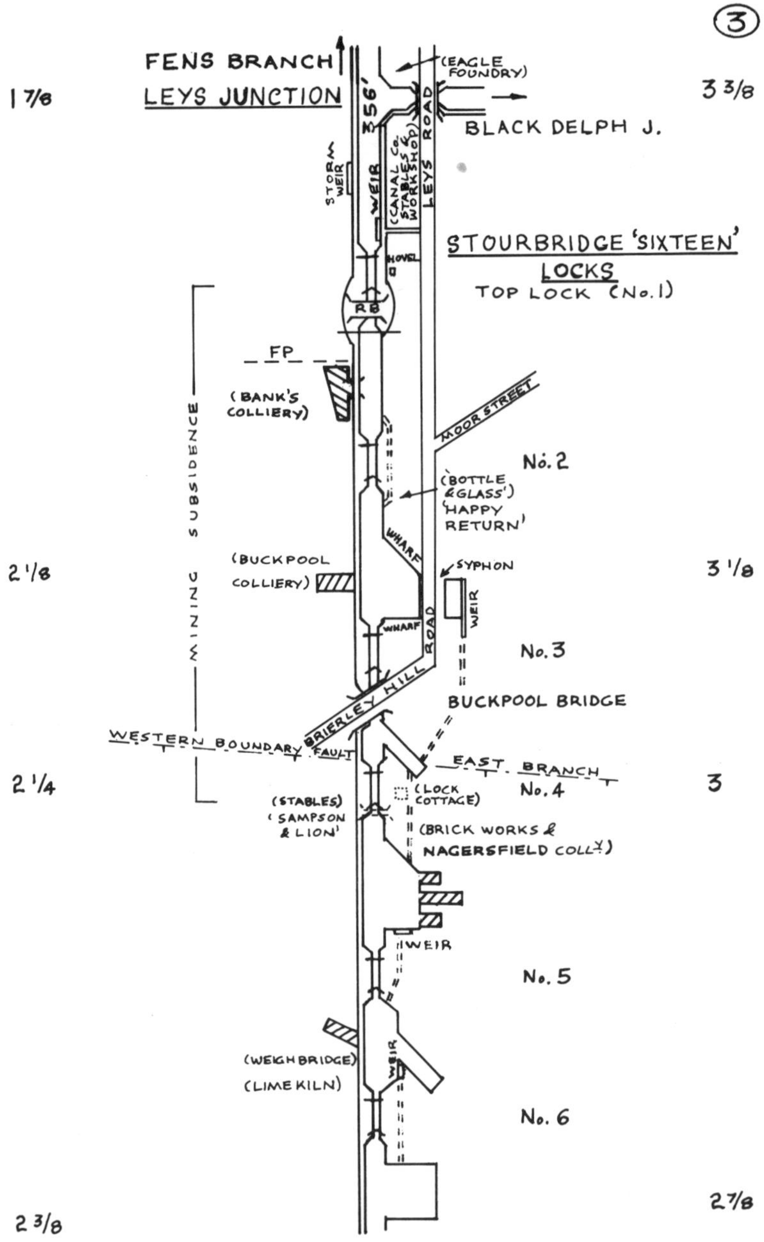
③
FENS BRANCH
LEYS JUNCTION
1 7/8
3 3/8
(EAGLE FOUNDRY)
BLACK DELPH J.
356'
STORM WEIR
WEIR
(CANAL Co. STABLES & WORKSHOP)
LEYS ROAD
STOURBRIDGE 'SIXTEEN' LOCKS
TOP LOCK (No.1)
HOVEL
RB
FP
(BANK'S COLLIERY)
MINING SUBSIDENCE
MOOR STREET
No. 2
('BOTTLE & GLASS')
'HAPPY RETURN'
WHARF
(BUCKPOOL COLLIERY)
2 1/8
SYPHON
3 1/8
WEIR
WHARF
ROAD
No. 3
BRIERLEY HILL
BUCKPOOL BRIDGE
WESTERN BOUNDARY FAULT
EAST BRANCH
2 1/4
3
(LOCK COTTAGE)
No. 4
(STABLES) 'SAMPSON & LION'
(BRICK WORKS & NAGERSFIELD COLLY)
WEIR
No. 5
(WEIGHBRIDGE)
(LIME KILN)
WEIR
No. 6
2 3/8
2 7/8

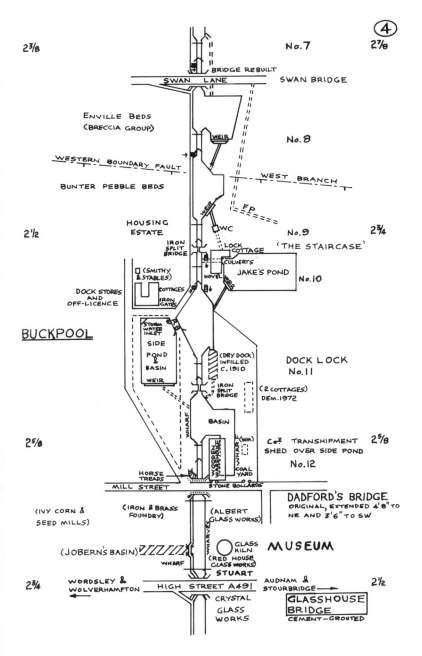

④

2³⁄₈

2⁷⁄₈

No. 7

BRIDGE REBUILT

SWAN LANE — SWAN BRIDGE

ENVILLE BEDS
(BRECCIA GROUP)

WEIR

No. 8

WESTERN BOUNDARY FAULT

WEST BRANCH

BUNTER PEBBLE BEDS

WEIR

FP

2½

2¾

HOUSING
ESTATE

WC

No. 9

'THE STAIRCASE'

IRON
SPLIT
BRIDGE

LOCK
COTTAGE

CULVERTS

(SMITHY
& STABLES)

HOVEL

JAKE'S POND

No. 10

COTTAGES

DOCK STORES
AND
OFF-LICENCE

IRON
GATES

BUCKPOOL

STORM
WATER
INLET

SIDE
POND
& BASIN

(DRY DOCK)
INFILLED
C. 1910

DOCK LOCK
No. 11

WEIR

IRON
SPLIT
BRIDGE

(2 COTTAGES)
DEM. 1972

WHARF

BASIN

2⁵⁄₈

(WM)

WHARF

Cᵒˣ TRANSHIPMENT
SHED OVER SIDE POND

No. 12

2⁵⁄₈

HORSE
TREADS

COAL
YARD

MILL STREET

STONE BOLLARDS

DADFORD'S BRIDGE
ORIGINAL, EXTENDED 4'8" TO
NE AND 3'6" TO SW

(IVY CORN &
SEED MILLS)

(IRON & BRASS
FOUNDRY)

(ALBERT
GLASS WORKS)

GLASS
KILN

MUSEUM

(JOBERN'S BASIN)

WHARF

(RED HOUSE
GLASS WORKS)

STUART

2¾

WORDSLEY &
WOLVERHAMPTON

HIGH STREET A491

AUDNAM &
STOURBRIDGE →

2½

CRYSTAL
GLASS
WORKS

GLASSHOUSE
BRIDGE
CEMENT-GROUTED

2 3/4

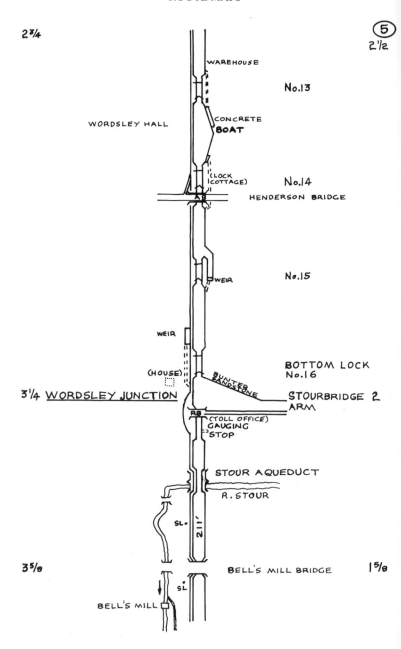

WAREHOUSE

No.13

WORDSLEY HALL

CONCRETE
BOAT

(LOCK
COTTAGE)

No.14

A B

HENDERSON BRIDGE

WEIR

No.15

WEIR

BOTTOM LOCK
No.16

(HOUSE)

BUNTER
SANDSTONE

3 1/4 <u>WORDSLEY JUNCTION</u>

STOURBRIDGE 2
ARM

RB (TOLL OFFICE)
GAUGING
STOP

STOUR AQUEDUCT

R. STOUR

SL

2 11'

3 5/8

BELL'S MILL BRIDGE

1 5/8

SL

BELL'S MILL

48

⑥

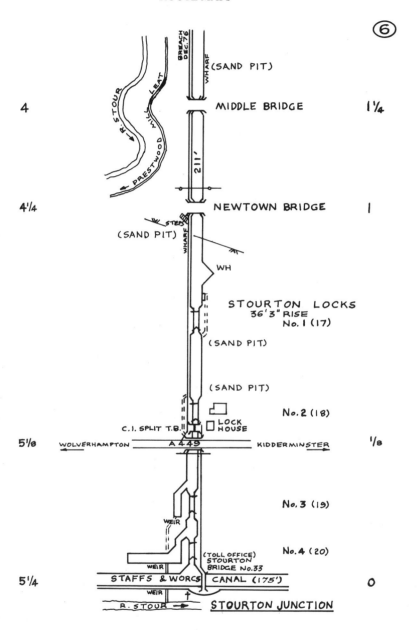

4

4¼

5⅛

5¼

(SAND PIT)

MIDDLE BRIDGE

211'

NEWTOWN BRIDGE

(SAND PIT)

STEPS

WH

STOURTON LOCKS
36'3" RISE
No. I (17)

(SAND PIT)

(SAND PIT)

No. 2 (18)

LOCK HOUSE

C. I. SPLIT T.B.

WOLVERHAMPTON   A 449   KIDDERMINSTER

No. 3 (19)

WEIR

No. 4 (20)

(TOLL OFFICE)
STOURTON
BRIDGE No. 33

WEIR

STAFFS & WORCS CANAL (175')

WEIR

R. STOUR

STOURTON JUNCTION

1¼

1

⅛

0

49

Stourbridge Branch

⑦

0

STOURTON J.
3 M.

HO·(¯)

WORDSLEY JUNCTION

LEYS J.
1 3/8 M.

1 3/8

GAUGING
STOP
COTT. (¯)

SST

STOURBRIDGE
'SIXTEEN'
BOTTOM LOCK

HOUSING
ESTATE

LONGBOAT LANE BRIDGE

THE JUNCTION

WEIR
SL

WHARF

AUDNAM BROOK

GLASSWORKS
TUDOR CRYSTAL

RIVER STOUR

1/4

(GLASSWORKS)
BOILERWORKS

JUNCTION ROAD

1 1/8

SST

CHUBBS BRIDGE

(AUDNAM
IRON AND
BRASS
FOUNDRY)

WHARF

21'

WHARF

(DIAL
FOUNDRY
AND
GLASSWORKS)

COALBOURN BROOK

(STOURBRIDGE
& DISTRICT W.B.)
PUMPING
STATION

(WH)

1/2

WOLLASTON

ROAD

7/8

COALBOURN BROOK BRIDGE

(WOLLASTON
EDGE-TOOL
MILLS)

WEIR

SST

DRY
DOCK

SL

WH

(STABLES)
(CRANE)

WHARF

RIVERSIDE HOUSE

1

STOURBRIDGE
IRONWORKS
(JOHN BRADLEY & Co)

RB

RB

JOHN BRADLEY
COALBROOKDALE
TITAN WORKS

3/8

(LIMEKILNS)

STOP NARROWS

(OLD WHARF
SAWMILLS)

BONDED
WAREHOUSE
& CANAL Co.
OFFICES

CANAL ST

WHARVES

WHARVES

WHS

WH

OLD
WHARF
ROAD

1 3/8

STOURBRIDGE

'MOORINGS TAVERN'

0

HIGH STREET

STOURBRIDGE
TRADING ESTATE

(GWR INTERCHANGE
BASIN)

(GASWORKS)

50

Fens Branch

(BAGGERIDGE, ASHWOOD BASIN, ETC.)

(PENSNETT RAILWAY)

(CORBYN'S HALL)

FENS POOL

(OLD PARK COLL.)

MIDDLE POOL

(ROUND OAK STEEL WORKS)

(WALLOWS COLL.)

0

7/8

GROVE POOL

(COAL WHARVES)

(COAL WHARVES)

WIDE WATERS

(FISH PIT, BROMLEY COLL.)

1/4

PENSNETT ROAD B4179

(HAY WHARF/ BROCKMOOR BRIDGE)

CULVERTED

5/8

(BROMLEY IRONWORKS)

(COLL. BASIN)

SL.

WHARVES

356'

(BROMLEY COLL.)

BROCKMOOR

1/2

CRESSET LANE

HAYWOOD BRIDGE

3/8

(COOKLEY WORKS)

(G.W.R. KINGSWINFORD BR.)

STOURBRIDE EXTENSION

(SIDINGS)

(IRON & TIN PLATE WORKS)

5/8

(SHED)

RB

BROCKMOOR JUNCTION

1/4

(GUILLOTINE) (BROMLEY LOCK)

(COTT.)

(LEYS IRON FOUNDRY)

(BRICK & TILE WORKS)

(COKE OVENS)

(ALBERT WORKS)

WHARF

LEYS ROAD

LEYS BRIDGE

7/8

LEYS JUNCTION

BLACK DELPH JUNCTION

0

STOURTON JUNCTION

3 3/8 MLS.

1 7/8 MLS.

51

Stourbridge Extension Canal

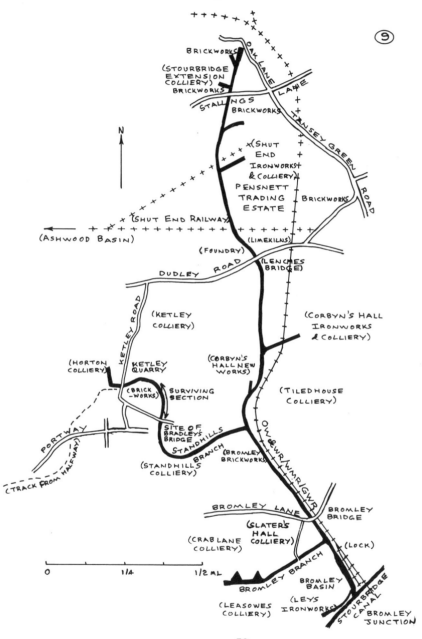

⑨

BRICKWORKS

(STOURBRIDGE EXTENSION COLLIERY) BRICKWORKS

OAK LANE

STALLINGS BRICKWORKS

TANSEY GREEN ROAD

N

x (SHUT END IRONWORKS & COLLIERY)

PENSNETT TRADING ESTATE

BRICKWORKS

x (SHUT END RAILWAY)

(ASHWOOD BASIN)

(LIMEKILNS)

(FOUNDRY)

(LENCHES BRIDGE)

DUDLEY ROAD

KETLEY ROAD

(KETLEY COLLIERY)

(CORBYN'S HALL IRONWORKS & COLLIERY)

(HORTON COLLIERY)

KETLEY QUARRY

(CORBYN'S HALL NEW WORKS)

(TILEDHOUSE COLLIERY)

(BRICK -WORKS)

SURVIVING SECTION

SITE OF BRADLEY'S BRIDGE

STANDHILLS BRANCH

(BROMLEY BRICKWORKS)

OW & WR / WMR / GWR

PORTWAY

(STANDHILLS COLLIERY)

(TRACK FROM HALFWAY)

BROMLEY LANE

BROMLEY BRIDGE

(SLATER'S HALL COLLIERY)

(CRAB LANE COLLIERY)

(LOCK)

0   1/4   1/2 ML

BROMLEY BRANCH

BROMLEY BASIN

STOURBRIDGE CANAL

(LEASOWES COLLIERY)

(LEYS IRONWORKS)

BROMLEY JUNCTION

Appendix

THE STAFFORDSHIRE & WORCESTERSHIRE CANAL SOCIETY

A feature of the age in which we live is that whenever part of our heritage is threatened with annihilation, then a group of preservationists immediately band together to save it. Canals are no exception and many have societies which were formed in this way. Once the threat of closure has been averted, the societies aim towards conservation rather than preservation and make a valuable contribution towards the life of their adopted canals. They encourage greater usage, promote interest among their members and the general public, assist towards maintenance, and act as 'watchdogs' to ensure that nothing interferes with these activities. The importance of the part played by canal societies in the recent history of our waterways should not be underestimated and this is particularly true of the Stourbridge. The story of the Staffordshire & Worcestershire Canal Society is told here by Alan T. Smith, Vice-President of the Society.

* * *

During and immediately after the Second World War, the inland navigations of this country steadily deteriorated, some becoming derelict or unnavigable and subject to Acts of Closure. The Staffs & Worcs Canal was threatened in 1959, when the Bowes Committee of Inquiry recommended that it should no longer be kept navigable. Although the Inland Waterways Association pursued an active campaign nationally to stop the decay and develop waterways to the full, it was felt that a local body was needed to safeguard the future of the Staffs & Worcs. In 1959 a small group of enthusiasts from the Wolverhampton area formed the Staffordshire & Worcestershire Canal Society, a voluntary, non-profit making organisation. Its main aim, as stated in its constitution, is 'to advocate the development and maintenance of the waterway and the promotion of the waterway to its fullest usage in conjunction with other Midland navigations'. The last phrase proved to highly significant, for some of the Society's important campaigns have been associated with adjoining waterways, such as the Stourbridge, whose abandonment would have seriously affected the usefulness of the Staffs & Worcs.

In order to increase membership and provide a working fund, the

Society introduced various social functions, such as indoor meetings during the winter months and narrow-boat trips to places of interest, activities which have since retained their popularity. The monthly *Broadsheet* started as a single sheet, as its name suggests, and has grown into an illustrated magazine of many pages, though it is still produced entirely by voluntary effort. Every member receives a copy and it is also circulated widely to the Press and Public Libraries, who frequently quote from it. Since it was formed in 1959, the Society has widened its activities to include the provision of lectures to various organisations and the establishment of a Society shop and exhibition stand that are available for public events.

The early excursions, such as one by a horse-drawn narrow boat on the Cannock Extension Canal, were purely for pleasure, but these developed into trips aimed at drawing attention to canals threatened with closure. Cruises of this type were made through Toll End locks and along the Titford Branch, both part of the Birmingham system. A major effort was made in 1960 when a fleet of boats started from Brades locks, Oldbury, cruised through Netherton tunnel and returned through Dudley tunnel which was then in danger of being closed. In spite of this effort, Dudley tunnel was closed to navigation the following year. However, after strong pressure was brought to bear by the Society, the British Transport Commision allowed a sight-seeing trip through the tunnel to take place. Public interest was aroused to such an extent that the Dudley Tunnel Preservation Society was formed. This later became the Dudley Canal. Trust, through whose efforts the tunnel was reopened to navigation on 21st April 1973.

In 1961 the Society was alarmed by the proposal of the Commission to close the Stourbridge Canal, a vital link between the Staffs & Worcs and the Birmingham Canal Navigations. The canal had already deteriorated to the point of being barely navigable and in October 1961 a fleet of boats attempted to reach Stourbridge town, falling short of the objective by about ½ mile, despite the strenuous efforts of their crews. The Society offered to carry out voluntary work on the canal, but the Commission refused to co-operate and the Society decided to join with the Inland Waterways Association in holding a National Rally of Boats at Stourbridge in 1962. The preparations were arduous and there was bitter antagonism between the organisers and the Commission. This came to a head with the historic incident of a dragline that had been brought to clear the canal in defiance of the Commission's ruling on the matter. Nationwide publicity resulted, there was a record attendance at the rally and the canal remained open. Then, during the mid 1960s, the Stourbridge 'Sixteen' locks were restored jointly by BWB and the Society. The restoration of the flight, and the events which preceded it, are described in chapter 6.

Meanwhile, It was felt that the aims and activities of the Society merited its recognition as a charity, and it became registered as such by the Charity Commissioners in 1965. As a consequence of the Transport Act of 1968, the Staffs & Worcs Canal and the main line of the Stourbridge were included in the 'Cruiseway' system. The Society has since assisted the Board with such work as the painting of lock gates, tree felling and towpath maintenance. The condition of the canal has continued to improve and usage has increased, so that there are now about twenty boats per mile along the Staffs & Worcs, making it one of the most popular cruising canals of the entire system.

During the 1970s the Society drew attention to the historic importance of the canal and its associated buildings. Following a report produced by the Society in 1974, the Staffs & Worcs, aside from a short length in Wolverhampton, was designated a Conservation Area. This was later extended to include much of the Stourbridge Canal, including the 'Town Arm'. Successful campaigns prevented the destruction of several important buildings, including the Tontine Hotel at Stourport, toll offices at Great Haywood and Stourton and Dadford's Shed, Wordsley. The greatest achievement in this field was of course the preservation of the Bonded Warehouse and canal-office complex at Stourbridge. In recent years members have installed 'finger posts', made from old lock balance beams, at each end of the five junctions along the canal, including Stourton (page 21) and have erected name boards at the locks.

The Society has been active in encouraging riparian authorities, both along the Staffs & Worcs and on neighbouring canals, to develop the adjoining land to the best advantage. Efforts have also been made to stimulate public interest in waterways and to encourage full use by the local populace of the many leisure pursuits available on canals. Social activities include a meeting held on the second Monday of each month at Bradmore, Wolverhampton. Trips continue to be a regular attraction and these are usually held during the early summer, visiting parts of the system that are not readily accessible to members who do not own boats. An annual gathering of boats is held during the Spring Bank Holiday and there are spring and autumn cruises to various parts of the Midland canal network.

The activities of the Staffordshire & Worcestershire Canal Society have benefited all who use the canal and its adjoining waterways, whether they boat, fish or just walk along the towpath. Anyone interested in improving the amenities of our canals for all to enjoy would be most welcome as a member of the Society.

Index

Page numbers set in **heavy type** indicate principal references to places and items along the canal. Numbers set in *italics* refer to illustrations (plate numbers).

Acts of Parliament: Civic Amenities Act (1974) 41; Dudley C. Act (1776) 6; Provisional Order Act (1894) 37; Stourbridge C. Act (1776) 6,11,23,29; (1935) 30; Stourbridge Extension C. Act (1837) 7,34; Transport Act (1968) 55,41

Agenoria (locomotive) 26

Amblecote 27

Amblecote UDC 40,42

Aqueduct, Stour 7,19,*18*

Audnam 27

Audnam brook 13,14,28

Bantock, Thomas 17,21,*3,12*

Basins: Brockmoor (Wide Waters) 29,30; Bromley 10,33,*26*;Delph (EJ&J Pearson) 9,*3*; interchange 10,17, 21,33,37,22,*26-28*; Joburn's 18; Stourbridge 10; Stourton 20,21; Wheeley's 10-12,*4-6*

Birmingham Canal Navigations (BCN) 6,7,9,14,15

Bonded Warehouse **23-24**,42,55,*20,21,23*

Bond's Folly 15,35

Bowes Committee 53

Bradley, John 25

Breaches: Bell's Mill 19,*19*; Wheeley's basin 11,*5,6*

Brettell Lane 10,12

Brickworks: Bromley *29*; Clattershall 10; Delph (EJ&J Pearson) 9,*3*; George King Harrison 11,12,*5*; Himley Firebrick 37; Hinton, Perry & Davenhill 36; Ketley 36; Nagersfield 14,15; Price Pearson 13; Stourbridge Glazed Brick & Tile 37

Bridges: Bell's Mill 19; Bowen's 10; Brierley 12; Bromley 34, *26,29*; Chubb's 27; Coalbournbrook 26,27; Dadford's 17; Farmer's 13; Glasshouse 17,18,*13*; Hay Wharf

(Brockmoor) 29,36,*26*; Ketley Lane ('Bradley's') 36,*31,32* Lenches 37; Long 12; Longboat Lane 28; Middle 19; Newtown 19,*20*; Seven Dwellings 10; Swan Lane 15; Wollaston Road 27

Brierley Hill UDC 42

Brindley, James 5,*1*

British Transport Commission (BTC) 39,40,42,54

British Waterways Board (BWB) 24,40,41,54

Bromley 7

Bromley Branch 34,**35**,*26*

Buckpool 15-17

Bunter Pebble Beds 15,16,18,19,27

Bunter Sandstone 28

Canal Street (Stourbridge) 24,25,*21*

Cannock Extension C. (BCN) 54

Carriers: Bantock, Thomas 17,21,*3*; Clayton, Thomas (Oldbury) 24; Fellows, Morton & Clayton 24; Shropshire Union Canal Carrying Co. 24

Chainworks 11

Clayton, Thomas, (Oldbury) 24

Coal seams: Brooch 11; Thick 5,7, 10-13,27,30,34,35,*30*

Coalbourn brook 11,12,27

Coalbournbrook 26,27,42

Coalbrookdale 25

Collieries: Ash Tree 10; Bank's 14; Beanfield 12; Brettell Lane 12; Bretwell Hall 11; Bromley 30; Buckpool 14; Chapman's Field 13; Coal Leasows 35; Corbyn's Hall 37; Crab Lane 35; Delph 10; George King Harrison's 11; Harding's Field 10,11; Horton 36; Ketley 36; Little Meadow 35; Louse Park 10; Nagersfield 11,14,15; Oak Farm

34,37,*30*; Shut End 37; Slater's Hall 35; Springfield 13; Standhills 36,37; Tinker's Field 10, Turner's Lane 10; Wallows 30; Wheeley's 11
Concrete boats 18,27,*15*
Conservation Areas 8,14,19,39,41,42,55
Cresset Lane 30
Cruiseways 39,41,42
Dadford, Thomas, Jr 7,16,17,19
Dadford, Thomas, Sr 7
'Dadford's Shed' 17,55,*12*
Delph 6,7,9,14,23,27,*4*
Dock, The 16,*11*
Dry docks 17,26,42,*11*
Dudley & Ward, Lord (2nd) 5-7,26
Dudley Canal 6-9,13,14,17,23,*34*
Dudley Canal Trust 54
Dudley MBC 24
Dune Sands 19,24,27
Enville Beds 15
Etruria Marl: see Old Hill Marl
Faults: Brierley Hill Trough 9,12,13; Western Boundary 12,15,35,36
Fellows, Morton & Clayton 24
Fens Branch 13,14,**29-31**,34,35,*25*
Foster: Henry 25; James 25; William Orme 26
Fowler, William 12
Gasworks: Brierley Hill Gas Light 9; Stourbridge 24
Glassworks 10,17; Dial 27; London House 18; Red House 17,*13,34*; Stuart Crystal 17,*13*; Tudor Crystal 28; White House 18
Grand Union Canal 18
Great Western Railway (GWR) 11,17, 21,24,29,30,34,37,*22,24,26,29*
Guest's wharf 27
Harrison, George King 11
Hill & Smith 16
Inland Waterways Association (IWA) 39,40,53,54
Iron foundries: Brierley 12; Brockmoor 13; Dial 27; Eagle 13,29; Titan 24
Ironworks: Bradley, J 25,26,33,36, 37,*24,31*; Brierley 12; Brierley Hill 16; Bromley 30; Corbyn's Hall 8,33; Corbyn's Hall New Works 37; Foster & Orme 23; Leys (Lays) 33; Roberts & Cooper 11; Shut End 33,36,37; Stourbridge 25,26,*24*; Wheeley's 10
Ivy Mills 17
Jake's Pond 16
Junction Cottages 27
Junctions: Brockmoor *26*,27,29; Bromley *26*; Delph 9; Leys 13,**29**; Stourton

15,**21**,23,41,42,*33*; Wordsley **18,19**, 23,**28**,*17*
Keuper Marl 20
Ketley Road 35,*31*
Kingswinford 12,35
Kingswinford Branch (OW&WR/ GWR) 30,33,37,38,*26, 29*
Leys, The 6,9,13,14,23
Limekilns 13,24,35
Locks: Brades (BCN) 54; Delph (Dudley C.) 11,29; Jackson's Stop Lock 11,34, 37,*26*; Shed 7; 'Sixteen' (Wordsley) 6,**13-18**,28,29,30,35,40-42,*7-17,34,35*; Stourton **20,21**,28; 'The Staircase' 16,*9-11,34*; Toll End (BCN) 54
London & North Western Railway (L&NWR) 24
Lower High Street (Stourbridge) 24,*22, 23*
Lower Mottled Sandstone: see Dune Sands
Lunt, Comley & Pitt 37
Mining subsidence 8,11,14,37,*5-8*
Museums: Black Country 10,13,14,36,*31*; Gloucester Waterways 15,18,27
Oak Farm 7,30,34
Old Hill (Etruria) Marl 36
Oxford, Worcester & Wolverhampton Railway (OW&WR) 8,10,24,30,33, 38,*4,22,26,28,29*
Paddle gear: BCN 15,*7,9,10*; SNCo 15,16,20,*14,16*
Pensnett Chase 6,*2*
Pensnett coal concentration depot 37
Pensnett Railway 30,31
Pensnett Trading Estate 34,37
Pottery: Smith's 12
Public Houses: 'Barrel Inn' 24; 'Bottle & Glass' 14; 'Crooked House' ('Glynne Arms') 30,*34*; 'Fish Inn' 27; 'Moorings Tavern' 24; 'Sampson & Lion' 14; 'Swan' 15
Quarry: Ketley 36
Rastrick, John Urpeth 25
Remainder Waterways 41
Reservoirs 6,7,14,*2*; FensPool 30; Grove Pool 30, Middle Pool 30,31
Restoration 8,**39-42**,54,*34*
Riverside House 26
Roberts & Cooper 11
Sandpits 19,20,27
Sawmills, Old Wharf 24,*23*
Shropshire Canal Carrying Co 24
Shut End 7
Shut End (Kingswinford) Railway 7,26,33

Staffordshire & Worcestershire C. 16, 19-21,23,39,53-55,*1*

Staffordshire & Worcestershire Canal Society (S&WCS) 21,39,40,42,**53-55**

Standhills Branch **35,36**,37,*31*

Stewpony 21

Stour Navigation 5,19

Stour, river 5,7,13,18,20,24-26,28,*18*

Stourbridge 6,19,23,24,26,39,40,54,55,*1, 20-22*

Stourbridge & District Water Board 27

Stourbridge Arm: see S. Branch

Stourbridge Branch 18,19,**23-28**,36,39-42, 54,55,*20-24,32*

Stourbridge C.: Acts of Parliament 6,11,23,29,30; Cost 6; Dividend 8; Promoters 5,18; Proposed line 5,*1*; Survey 5,6,*2*; Notices 40, *33*; Restoration 8,**39-42**,54,*34*; Water supplies 27,29-31; see also Fens Branch and Stourbridge Branch

Stourbridge Extension C.: Act of Parliament 7,34; Cost 7; Decline and closure 36-38; Purchase by OW&WR 8; Water supplies 33,34; see also Bromley Branch and Standhills Branch

Stourbridge Lion (locomotive) 26

Stourbridge Navigation Co. 5,6,30,*14,16*; Offices 24,55,*21*; Seal *34*

Stourbridge Navigation Trust (SNT) 23,24,*21*

Stourbridge Rolling Mills 24

Stourbridge Wharf 23,24

Stourbridge, Wolverhampton & Birmingham Junction C. 7

Stourton 5,19,26,33,40,41

Subsidence: see mining subsidence

Thomas, Richard, & Baldwin (RTB) 21,29

Titford Branch (BCN) 54

Toll offices 18,21

Transhipment sheds: Bromley 33,34,*27, 28;* 'Dadford's' 17,55,*12*

Tunnels: Brettell Lane 12,*4*; Dudley 7,54; Netherton 54

Upper Mottled Sandstone 19

Weirs 13,20,28

West Midlands CC 24,42

Wheeley Bros 10

Wheeley, W.S. *4*

Whitworth, Robert 6,7

Wide Waters (Brockmoor basin) 11,30

Wordsley 6,17

Wordsley brook 14,18,30,33

Yarranton, Andrew 5

Young, Joseph 24